Sopranino

Other Sailing Classics

SEA STORIES by Joseph Conrad
ROUGH PASSAGE by R D Graham
THE CRUISE OF THE ALERTE by E F Knight
THE CRUISE OF THE KATE by E E Middleton
ACROSS THREE OCEANS by Conor O'Brien
SAILING ALONE AROUND THE WORLD by Joshua
    Slocum
ONCE IS ENOUGH by Miles Smeeton
ENDURANCE by Alfred Lansing
BECAUSE THE HORN IS THERE by Miles Smeeton
SURVIVE THE SAVAGE SEA by Dougal Robertson
THE LONG WAY by Bernard Moitessier
CAPE HORN: THE LOGICAL ROUTE by Bernard
    Moitessier
DESPERATE VOYAGE by John Caldwell
THE CRUISE OF THE AMARYLLIS by G H P
    Muhlhauser
THE SEA WAS OUR VILLAGE by Miles Smeeton

Sopranino

Patrick Ellam
and Colin Mudie

GRAFTON BOOKS
A Division of the Collins Publishing Group

LONDON GLASGOW
TORONTO SYDNEY AUCKLAND

Grafton Books
A Division of the Collins Publishing Group
8 Grafton Street, London W1X 3LA

First published by Rupert Hart-Davis Ltd 1954
This edition published by Grafton Books 1986

British Library Cataloguing in Publication Data

Ellam, Patrick
  Sopranino.
  1. Voyages and travels——1951– 2. Atlantic Ocean
  I. Title   II. Mudie, Colin
  910'.09163   G540

ISBN 0–246–12943–3

Printed in Great Britain by
Mackays of Chatham Ltd

TO ALL THOSE KIND PEOPLE WITHOUT WHOSE
ENCOURAGEMENT AND HELP THIS EXPEDITION
COULD NEVER HAVE BEEN COMPLETED

NOTE

Sopranino means, literally, *Little Soprano*, and refers to the smallest wind instrument in music. When we set out to produce the smallest possible seagoing sailing boat, it seemed appropriate to borrow the name for her.

Contents

ONE	In the Beginning	9
TWO	The Die is Cast	22
THREE	Building Up	34
FOUR	Southward Ho!	46
FIVE	Fair Wind to Africa	69
SIX	Over the Western Ocean	86
SEVEN	The Firgas Drinkers	108
EIGHT	Barbados	131
NINE	Windward Islands	144
TEN	Westward to Cuba	161
ELEVEN	Florida Reefs	176
	Epilogue	192
	The Technical Side	193

Illustrations

MAPS AND DIAGRAMS

The English Channel   15
Cutaway view of *Sopranino*   24
England to the Canary Islands   47
Atlantic Crossing   95
The West Indies   145
Florida Reefs   189

CHAPTER ONE

In the Beginning

The Situation—An Idea—Theta—Thames Estuary—The Hitch-Hiker—To France and Back in a Gale—The Information Comes in—A Longer Passage—The Customs Officer

IT WAS Colin's turn to cook breakfast and I was lying in my bunk, thinking over the things that wanted doing, while he went out on deck to read the log and see what the Good Lord had given us in the night.

'Hey', he called out, 'What day is it?'

I hurriedly looked in the log book.

'Friday', I said.

'Friday the what?' I looked again.

'Twenty-fifth. Fourteen days out.'

'Good.'

'Why?'

'The log's come up to the hundred.'

I looked in the book again. That would be 1400. A hundred miles a day since we started. Fine. Then I did a double take:

'Hey! That means we're half-way.'

'That's right.'

'Oh!'

I lay back in my bunk again and considered the matter. I never was very bright in the early mornings.

Half-way across the Atlantic Ocean. Fourteen hundred miles behind us lay the Canary Islands, off the coast of Africa, and fourteen hundred ahead lay the West Indies. I looked down to the end of the cabin, where there was a large pair of feet. I wiggled them. They were my own. The cabin was exactly 6 feet 6 inches long, tailored to fit two men, side by side.

I scrambled out into the hatch. When I stood on the keel, the cabin roof came up to my waist, while from there I could stretch out my arms and lay my hands over both sides of our

9

Sopranino

little boat at once. She was not very big, less than twenty feet long to be exact, but that was the point. We were out to prove that really small boats, so small that they could be trailed behind the family car and stored in the garage for the winter, could go anywhere on the sea in safety.

Over the years two distinct and separate types of sailing boat had developed: big solid craft, heavily built to withstand the enormous power of the sea, the very smallest of which weighed around two and a half tons, and small, lightly built boats such as dinghies and canoes that were generally considered unsafe outside harbours or estuaries except on fine days and under escort.

The heavy boats relied on the weight of their keels to right them if they were knocked down by a squall or a breaking sea, while in the little ones it was up to the crews to keep them upright by moving their own weight from side to side.

All attempts to produce very small seagoing boats had followed the general principle of scaling down the big fellows. The resulting boats had two main disadvantages. On the whole their performance was very poor, with a reputation for never getting anywhere, and as they still weighed at least a ton or two they were far too heavy to be taken home like a dinghy for maintenance, on a trailer behind the family car. And maintenance represents the greater part of the cost of running a boat.

After the war, around 1946, I had decided to attack the problem from the other angle: to produce a boat the size and weight of a dinghy, but modified so that it would be really safe at sea in any weather while retaining the dinghy's high speed and manoeuvrability. I believed that such a boat would be so light that it would ride right over the waves like a ping-pong ball without suffering any harm.

First of all I decided to make an experiment to determine just what were the limits to which we might go. For this I chose as a starting point one of the most extreme types of boat ever developed, the racing sailing canoe. These craft are about seventeen feet long, very light and narrow; decked in all over,

In the Beginning

they look rather like a large flat wooden cigar. They carry a lot of sail for their size and the only way that they can be persuaded to stay upright is for the crew of one man to sit on the end of a long plank projecting from the side, acting as a counterweight to the pressure of the wind on the sails.

They are probably the most tricky boats to handle of any, and in rough water they are just about the fastest. There were a couple of dozen of the one-man types in the world and at that time there was one two-seater belonging to a very well-known designer who had achieved considerable acclaim by performing the unusual feat of sailing her across the Channel. This was generally regarded as an exceptional performance by a slightly eccentric genius and not to be attempted by ordinary mortals.

Kenneth Gibbs, naval architect and boatbuilder, of Sunbury-on-Thames, had developed a two-man boat on the same lines and it had turned out to be exceptionally fast and moderately seaworthy, so I got him to build me a modified version of this type, 20 feet long and carrying even more than the usual amount of sail.

I called her *Theta* and she was equipped with four built-in buoyancy tanks, a compass, and lockers for navigation equipment, stores, and food. For a start we did without the plank, relying on our hanging right out over the side to keep her upright in strong winds.

She was completed in the late summer of 1948 and taken by trailer to Cornwall for trials. She turned out, as we had expected, to be extremely fast for her size, being able to hold her own against full-sized ocean racers. And at the same time she appeared to be a remarkably good sea-boat so long as her crew were really on their toes, though she reacted violently to the slightest touch of her controls, like a highly bred racehorse.

In the autumn of 1949 I decided really to set about finding just what she would and would not do. At the same time there was the interesting question of what the average crew could stand. This time we launched her at Brightlingsea, with the idea of making her fight her way down Channel against the prevailing southwesterly winds.

Sopranino

For the first trip, a matter of 30 miles across the Thames Estuary to Ramsgate, I took with me a friend, John Watson, who had had practically no sailing experience. We started out in a flat calm, drifting around among the shoals and sand banks with a thin watery sun trying its best to penetrate the swirling wreaths of fog, but such is the weather in those parts that before long it had developed into a light gale from the south, dead ahead.

Poor John was horribly seasick, so that it was the most he could do to hang on and wish he were dead. The seas came up and the night came down and the wind howled in the rigging, doing its best to push us back on to the bleak coast of Essex.

Theta behaved beautifully, taking the seas as they came, going over, under, or through them as the mood occurred to her, but never stopping and all the time working her way up, yard by yard towards our destination. By noon the next day we were safe in harbour, well pleased with the results of the first experiment.

Next week-end John was unable to make it, so I wandered down to Ramsgate to see if I could pick up a crew. I had decided to run her over to Boulogne, only about 40 miles away, but nobody seemed to want to go that way, so I paddled her out into the Outer Harbour and was quietly getting the sails and things ready when I noticed a young student sitting on the wall with a large rucksack beside him. I shouted across to him:

'You waiting for a boat?'

'I was looking for a lift to France.'

'Can you swim?'

'Yes.'

'I'll run you over. I'm going that way.'

'What! In that?'

'Yes.'

'O.K.'

'I'll come over.'

Theta had no motor, so I paddled and prodded my way across to him and slung his rucksack in the forward locker.

In the Beginning

His name was Bob Green, and he had never been in a boat before, but it turned out that he had been a fighter pilot in the R.A.F. I always use an R.A.F.-type steering compass and *Theta's* steering was rigged the same way as that in an aircraft, so I gave him the job of steering while I did everything else.

He turned out to be an ideal crew for an experimental run. He did exactly as he was told and did not know enough about what was going on either to argue or to be frightened. Also he was impervious to damp.

By the time we reached the French coast a good strong sou'wester had got up, piling the seas into great curling combers. Running in parallel to the coast towards Boulogne, we could see the people on the shore quite clearly each time we rose up on a wave, and then down we would go into the next trough and all the world would be sea again.

As we were perched precariously on the top of one particular breaker I remarked to Bob:

'You know, I bet fifty per cent of those people on the shore don't think we'll get there alive.'

He waited until his head came up out of the foam of the breaker that had just collapsed around us, blew out a mouthful of salt water, and said:

'Well, as a matter of fact, old boy, fifty per cent of the people on this boat don't think so either.'

Soon after dark we arrived off Boulogne. There is a sunken sea wall on the northern side which is no thing to hit at a time like that, but it would have meant another hour's sailing to go around it and we were cold and wet and hungry, so we ran straight at it, pulled up the centre-board and rudder, which are the only things that stick out underneath, and shot over it into the harbour.

Inside we found a large British yacht, whose owner invited us aboard, filled us with hot food, and gave us a dry bunk each for the night.

Next morning we strolled through the docks into the bomb-blasted remains of the town. Ordinarily you would regard it as a pretty miserable sort of place, but when you have arrived

13

there on a sort of marine roller-skate you think that it is quite the most romantic spot and feel as though you have conquered it personally. Such are the joys of the game.

We had an early lunch in a local café and then set out for the return trip to England. It was just about one o'clock when we slid out through the breakwaters in an almost flat calm. The previous day's wind had gone but there were big oily rollers coming in from the westward and the ominous leaden sky held every sign of a real stinker of a storm brewing. The gale warnings were up and the big yachts were waiting in port to see what would happen, but we had to be back at work on Monday morning, so we shortened sail and lay heaving on the rollers awaiting events.

Then suddenly it came. Out of the west. A light puff that steadily increased in force until within half an hour it was blowing really hard. Our course lay to the northwest, to Folkestone some 26 miles away, and as the wind got up it backed around to the southwest as I had hoped it would do, leaving us with the wind on our beam, skimming along the length of the troughs and crests of the seas.

Obviously there was a limit to what this little boat would stand, and equally obviously this storm was going to cook up into something really big. The thing was rapidly getting interesting. *Theta* was skimming over the waves like a scalded cat, barely seeming to touch the water half the time while the visibility was closing in behind us, leaving us alone in an unfriendly world of sea and clouds and flying spray.

If we could keep this speed up and if nothing broke, I reckoned that we could make Folkestone Harbour before it got too much for her. Provided we did hit Folkestone. If not we should be marooned somewhere off the cliffs of Dover in a rising gale, a situation that I regarded as highly undesirable.

Navigating such a small boat under these conditions is no easy task. Everything—charts, notebooks, tables—that you need to work with is subjected to a continuous drenching in salt water at a high velocity, which renders it a useless mass of pulp in a few seconds. Nor can you plot your course with any

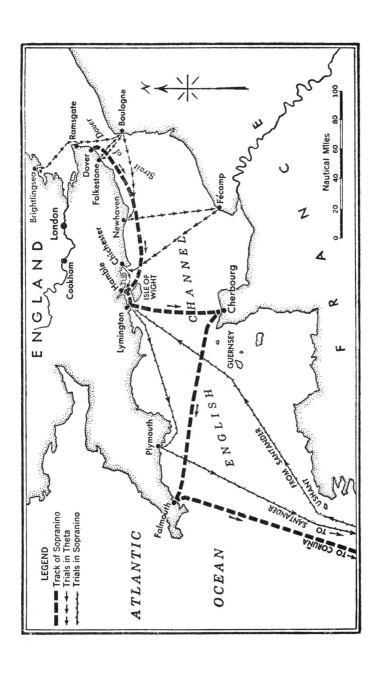

Sopranino

accuracy in advance as you can never say for certain in a sailing boat at what speed or even in which direction you will be going a couple of hours ahead.

I had worked out a theory for these conditions, in the peace and quiet of my armchair at home. Broadly, it consisted of starting off on a course based on our estimated speed and direction, with appropriate allowances for the tides. Then, when I reckoned we were half-way across, I estimated what speed we had actually made and in which direction, estimated what the wind and sea would do in the next part and what that would enable us to do, and consulted a typewritten table that I had prepared, bound up in plastic against the spray, that would tell me how to alter our course to allow for previous and future variations and take us straight to our destination. Now to see if my theory was going to work.

Soon we were half-way, consulted our tables, set the new course and hung on. As a matter of fact there was very little else that we could do at that stage of the game. Better to concentrate on keeping the boat on her feet and in one piece.

Visibility had closed in to a few miles all around us and the wind was still rising, working the seas up all the time and occasionally taking the tops off them in a long line of flying spray. The time came when we should see land, and the usual anxious look-out and soul-searching by the navigator. Had I made a mistake? Nothing that we could do about it now, anyway. Just hang on and hope.

Then a smudge of grey in the murk ahead. Cliffs. And a valley. And a sea wall and cranes. Folkestone. We were on target.

Closing in, we crossed the shipping lane. Rusty old tramps, some beating and banging their way into the storm, sending clouds of spray high into the air, and some running before it, rolling and wallowing, their propellers thrashing the water as their noses went down into the hollows.

'Out of our way, you ships. Stand aside. We are in sail.'

Soon we were rushing into the harbour, black thunderclouds closing in behind us and the calm water under the sea wall ahead. Inside the tide was out, exposing vast areas of mud. No stopping her at that speed, so we ran her straight up on to the mud, leaped over the side, and stood there holding her like a toy boat, with her sails flapping and banging in the wind.

I turned to Bob:

'What time?'

'Five past four.'

'Nice run. We're in time for tea.'

Three hours and five minutes. Lunch in France and tea in England. A stinker of a gale. The navigation had worked and the boat had held together. The information was coming in nicely.

Late that night in London the wind was howling in the trees and we heard that several of the big ocean racers in the Fastnet Race had been forced to retire for stress of weather.

All that week the gale continued and the following Friday evening Bob, who was rather fascinated by the whole business, came down with me to Folkestone for the next stage, a rather longer trip to Boulogne and back to Newhaven.

During the night the wind eased off and on Saturday morning we had a nice sail over to Boulogne, to find all the big yachts still bottled up there waiting for the weather, while we had been over to England, done a week's work and come back. Maybe little boats could be reliable.

A quick lunch in France and we were off on the 60-odd-mile hop to Newhaven. A lovely evening, sailing over smooth seas, straight down the path of gold thrown on the water by the setting sun, but as night fell the wind left us, becalmed somewhere off the English coast, dripping and damp and still.

We threw out our little anchor, dropped the sails that were doing no good where they were, and rigged them over ourselves as a sort of tent. All that night we writhed and cursed in the discomfort of trying to lie down and get some sleep in a boat that was never meant to be lain down in and slept in.

About four in the morning life was at a low ebb. We were tired and cold and damp and miserable. There was no means of heating any food so we had a sandwich each. The results

Sopranino

were immediate and surprising. We felt very much better and actually warmer. We decided that it must have been the butter that did the trick, remembering that on Arctic expeditions fats have a high place in the diet. Thus one finds out the strangest things in the most unexpected places.

But it was becoming obvious that if the boat were to keep going for more than two or three days the crew must be kept fit, so that it would be most important in any future boat to pay careful attention to their basic needs for hot food and somewhere dry and warm to sleep.

The next day the sun came out and the wind came up and we had another pleasant sail along the English coast until nightfall, when we were once again becalmed, this time a mile or two from Newhaven Harbour, our destination.

So out came the paddles, and about midnight we drifted into port, the third experiment completed. Apart from the main things, each experiment had yielded its quota of little titbits of information which, taken together, were to point the way towards future development.

The next week-end Bob was tied up. To be more accurate he was in the local jail for stowing away in the baggage compartment of a transatlantic aircraft to go and see his girl friend in Canada. Definitely an enterprising type.

However, he sent down a friend of his called Don, who thought that it might be fun to have a shot at this sailing business, so on Friday night we caught the train to the coast and immediately set out for Fécamp, some 66 miles to the south.

This time the wind blew steadily right through the night, so that by morning we were well out in the middle of the Channel. Out there, over twenty miles from the nearest land, sailing along in a smart breeze, we began to realise that we really did belong. That we could go up forward, lie on our stomachs and admire the greeny blue of the sea, or lean over and grab a piece of seaweed or maybe the odd cuttlefish as we passed it. Or even do circles and figures-of-eight for the sheer joy of it.

We were suspended in a strange world of infinite time and space and we had become a part of it. Not just a boat on the

In the Beginning

sea, but two people, with their boat, in it. A ship in the midst of the sea.

And we began to try tricks. It was tiring always to have to lean out to windward to balance the weight of the wind on the sails and I had heard of a device called a trapeze, consisting of a kind of sling in which you could sit, suspended by a wire from the masthead. With one of these you could swing your weight further out and sit in comfort, they said. So I borrowed Don's belt, tied it to a spare line that we kept handy to haul the sail up with in case the regular one should break, sat in the thing, and out I went.

At first it seemed horribly unstable, until I found the knack of keeping my feet spread well apart on the outside of the boat, and then I found that it was perfectly delightful. You could hang there on your rope in the attitude of a man cleaning a window on a high building, swinging along over the waves and looking down on the boat cutting her way through the water below you, while the other person, relieved of the strain of keeping the boat upright, could sit at his ease and steer in comfort.

After a while I came in and sent Don out to try it, and we took it in turns for a while. And then I did a silly thing. I was wearing oilskin waterproof trousers, sitting in the trapeze with my feet well apart, when the wind suddenly eased off for a moment. The side of the boat dipped down into the waves and before I realised what was happening the forward trouser leg was acting as a scoop, sending a powerful stream of water up my right leg and down the left one, where it ran out like a garden hose.

A silly thing that could have been avoided by tying string or possibly a rubber band around the bottom of each leg, but it did bring home to us how easily a real disaster could happen, suddenly and unexpectedly at any time, for lack of forethought.

The sea has no mercy. It is a place where vast elemental forces rule supreme, and he who sets out to sail over it is setting out to tame those forces, to make them do his bidding and take him safely to the place where he would be. But let him make

Sopranino

just one mistake and he will find that they are ever ready and waiting to rise up and destroy him.

Just after dark, as we approached Fécamp, the wind came around behind us and blew up a little, so that we came rushing in out of the darkness towards the lights of the town, riding the waves like a surfboard. And then suddenly we were in the harbour and all was peace and quiet, with all the lights along the quayside reflected in the smooth, still water and the sounds of people singing and dogs barking drifting across it to us. What a way to arrive in a foreign land!

Deep in the far corner of the little harbour we found an old fishing boat lying quietly at rest after its day's work, with no one abroad, so we tied up to it and curled up gratefully on its hard decks with our sail over us for a cover, for a night's rest.

Next morning we dug out the local customs officer, who politely refused to inspect us, had a quick meal ashore, and set off home again: 85 miles, this time, to Itchenor.

The run back was uneventful until we reached the English coast. You can always tell where England is. Just look for a long line of some kind of nasty weather along the horizon and you may be sure that there it is.

This time it was fog. Thick banks of it, with steamers honking past us, invisible and ominous. And, of course, no wind. But *Theta* kept drifting slowly along over the still, smooth waters. Once we made out a grey shape ahead and almost immediately we glided past a large sailing yacht, drifting helplessly in circles for lack of wind. He gave us a hail: 'Hey, where do you get your wind from?' and was lost in the fog behind us. Small, light boats with large sails have their advantages.

Then, quite suddenly, we came out of it, like sailing out of the side of a nebulous mountain, and there was Chichester Harbour ahead. Soon we were in the harbour and sailing up to Itchenor Creek, where we lifted *Theta* out of the water, carried her up the shore, and put her in the rack with the dinghies, a huge yellow quarantine flag flying from her tiny crosstrees to indicate that we had arrived from a foreign land.

In the Beginning

The customs officer came along the path, dismounted, leaned his bicycle against the wall, and approached us with some hesitation. Finally he said:

'Excuse me, sir, but is that meant to be a Q flag?'

We hastened to assure him that it was, and he sat down on the grass and solemnly cleared our papers.

In four successive week-ends we had covered 30, 66, 86, and 151 sea miles, regardless of weather and on schedule. We had crossed the Channel six times on our flimsy craft and learned a great deal. We were ready for the next stage.

CHAPTER TWO

The Die is Cast

Sopranino Is Conceived—Building on the Thames—Launching—Seven Hours on a
Trapeze—The Race to Spain—Junior Offshore Group—The Decision Is Made

A COUPLE of weeks later I went down to Itchenor and sailed *Theta* down the Solent to Lymington where Laurent Giles, the leading English designer of ocean racers, has his office.

It was a fine sunny morning when I strolled up the picturesque little street and into his bow-windowed office. I wandered in in my sailing clothes—tennis shoes, an old pair of skiing trousers, and a roll-neck sweater—and asked to speak to Mr Giles.

To my surprise I was shown straight in to see him and found myself in the presence of a tall, charming man who looked more like an artist than a designer, with his long hair and bow tie and casual manner.

I told him of my theory, of the experiments that we had made and the conclusions that we had drawn. Then I outlined my idea for a new boat, the same length as *Theta* but a few inches wider, to have a small cabin in which the man off watch could sleep in some comfort and a stove on which hot food could be cooked. With these advantages I believed that we would be able to keep the sea for days on end and go much longer distances.

All this time he had been looking at me with a quizzical smile, occasionally asking a question, and I began to wonder how mad he thought I was. Then, to my delight, he offered to design the boat for me, and *Sopranino* was conceived.

Immediately we got down to the details: questions of weights, sizes of sails, details of construction, and all the thousand and one small details which must be most carefully considered in a boat that is going out to face the sea for any length of time.

Talking about the sizes of the sails, I mentioned that I felt that a certain jib should be about sixty square feet. He looked up at me:

'Wouldn't sixty-two be better?'

The man knew his business and was already way ahead of me. I went home to await results.

A week or two later a large package arrived through the post. It was the preliminary drawings. One glance was enough to show that he had understood and appreciated exactly what was required.

I made notes on the plans of various modifications that I felt should be made and sent them back to him. When they came back to me I took them to Captain John H. Illingworth, R.N., then Commodore of the Royal Ocean Racing Club and one of the leading authorities in the world on the equipment and handling of sailing boats.

More suggestions, more modifications, and at last the final plans were drawn. Now to choose a builder.

In construction, and indeed in hull form, *Sopranino* was to be, in effect, a rather long narrow racing dinghy. So I went into the question of who built the best racing dinghies and finally settled on the Wootten brothers of Cookham Dene.

So one winter's day found me driving down through the countryside to their yard on the edge of Quarry Wood. From the car there was nothing to see, beyond a small sign saying 'Woottens' sticking up over a low hedge; then as I went through the little wooden gate I looked down a steep path that winds through the woods to the banks of the Thames below. And here and there, clinging to the precipitous slope, I made out a number of apparently unrelated sheds and huts of all shapes and sizes and colours: the yard.

There I met the two brothers and their dozen or so craftsmen, men who had carried on the traditions of boat-building for generations and who took a real pride in their work. This was where I wanted *Sopranino* to be built.

I showed them the plans. By any standards she was revolutionary, looking more like a toy submarine than anything else; but the construction was straightforward and the magic

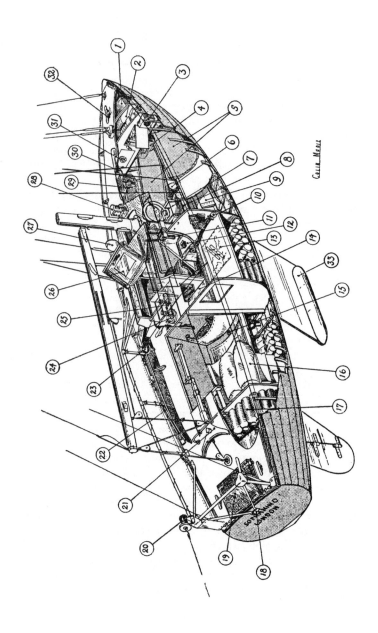

CECIL MILLS

1. Buoyancy bags in forepeak. 2. Personal lockers. 3. Radio loudspeaker. 4. Sextant. 5. Rubber mattresses in bunks. 6. Canvas chart roll. 7. D/F radio. 8. Working battery. 9. Paddles, spinnaker boom blade, under bunks. 10. Chronometer. 11. Hand bearing compass. 12. Vegetable bin cum wine locker (note bilge pump). 13. Chart table. 14. Seat with spare battery and water under. 15. Cockpit drain. 16. Sail bags, Ryvita, spare tinned food in side lockers. 17. Spare water cans, dry clothes, sea anchor in aft locker. 18. Crutch socket. 19. Aft hatch. 20. Log. 21. Self-steering quadrant and tiller. 22. Runner lever. 23. Snubbing winch. 24. Compass in middle of bridge deck. 25. Galley stove. 26. Main hatch with perspex window. 27. Ventilator. 28. Navigation light. 29. Net racks for seagoing clothes. 30. Barometer. 31. Thermometer. 32. Mooring cleat. 33. Lead weight on fin.

Sopranino is clinker built, her planks overlapping one another after the fashion of a dinghy. The planks themselves are of mahogany some three-eighths of an inch thick, barely thicker than a cigarette. Her ribs are of English oak, spaced four inches apart, and she is further strengthened by a series of bulkheads which, with the sides of the bunks and lockers and other interior woodwork, all combine to provide a light yet amazingly strong structure.

Her length over all is 19 feet 8 inches, 17 feet 6 inches on the water-line, while her beam is 5 feet 4 inches and she draws 3 feet 8 inches of water with her fin in place, the hull itself barely drawing 10 inches of water.

When she was built the hull weighed 410 pounds; but with the addition of 350 pounds of weight in the fin and the further weight of stores and equipment, her running weight is about half a ton. This compares with a boat of the same size but of normal construction, which would weigh about two tons: four times as much.

The mast is hollow, built of spruce, as are the booms. The fin is attached to the keel by a series of bolts so that it can be taken off for handling ashore or for trailing behind a car.

Below there are two full-sized bunks, each 6 feet 6 inches long, a galley with two stoves and a wash basin, and a full-sized chart table; the whole of the rest of the space in the ship is taken up with lockers to hold all the stores and equipment for long passages.

Sopranino

name Giles was in the corner of the plans, so they agreed to build her.

They had never built a seagoing vessel before, so I visited them twice a week during all the time that they were working, and every now and then Laurent Giles would call in to confer with them on the details.

They built her slowly and they built her carefully. They knew that men's lives would depend on every tiny detail of their work, not once but a hundred times, and they gave her of their best.

As I visited her through the spring of 1950 I would see her growing and developing slowly but surely. By midsummer she was nearly ready, but I had a small trick that I wanted to try out and time was getting short.

The final details seemed to take an eternity. And then, one fine evening I came back and she was gone from her place in the shed. I looked out over the river, and there she lay, floating light like a duck on the still waters of the Thames.

She could not be carried up the steep winding paths to the road above, so we had to tow her down the river to the nearest crane, where we lifted her out on to a light truck to take her down to Lymington and launch her in her proper element, the sea.

She was launched on a Friday evening at the beginning of August. Now for the trick that I had in mind. Every second year the Royal Ocean Racing Club has, as its longest and most important race, the Santander Race, in which the big yachts sail from Plymouth across the Channel, around Ushant, and away down across the Bay of Biscay to Spain.

Sopranino was far too small to be allowed to enter the race, since nobody had even considered the possibility of sailing clean across the Bay of Biscay in a decked-in dinghy, much less racing across. But I had had a quiet word with Captain Illingworth, who himself was a keen champion of the smaller ocean racers, and he had said that if we liked we could start with the big boys and sail down to Spain with them.

The race was due to start on August 8, barely a week after

The Die is Cast

Sopranino was launched, and from Plymouth, about 180 miles down Channel, to windward. We had no time to lose.

Early Saturday morning Tony Needham and I were aboard, making sheets and generally completing her gear, when Laurent Giles came down for a trial sail. She was of entirely revolutionary design and nobody could say for certain how she would sail, so Giles took the tiller as we tacked down the creek.

It was a bright sunny day with a nice breeze. We had our full sail set: mainsail, jib, and genoa staysail. Giles looked thoughtful at first, then smiled happily and said:

'Good. Would you like to take her?'

I took her. And nearly lost her in the first five minutes. There was a huge car ferry coming up the narrow creek with barely room for us to squeeze past it. I brought *Sopranino* up into the wind to clear another boat and flip! the jib backed, spun her round, and put her right in the ferry's path.

I could hear the clanging of bells aboard the huge monster as her master put his engines full astern to try and avoid running us under, while I did the only possible thing: put the helm over and completed the circle. Slowly we swung around, and in a moment we were clear and it was all over. I had made my first mistake. I had underestimated *Sopranino*. She was a sensitive and delicate wind instrument, to be played with light fingers.

Back at the jetty Giles wished us good luck and Tony came aboard with an armful of provisions for the trip to Plymouth. A farewell drink and we were off.

Out in the Channel, clear of the Isle of Wight, we soon got the feel of the little ship. She behaved beautifully, dancing lightly over the sunlit waves, making light of the choppy little seas that so often cause small boats to go up and down in the same hole. Not *Sopranino*. She slid gracefully over them, working her way up to windward towards Plymouth.

Compared with *Theta* she was a dream of comfort at sea. Two good dry bunks with proper ventilation, two cooking stoves, toilet, chart table, plenty of space for stores. What more could a sailor want?

Sopranino

For two nights and a day we sailed happily down Channel out of sight of land and on Monday morning we closed the coast at Start Point, to run up to Plymouth. The wind freshened to the point where the boat was hard pressed with the big jib up, but when we went to lower it we found that it would not come down. The halyard was jammed.

Fortunately I had brought a trapeze along, just in case we might need it, so we rigged it up and I went out and sat in it the way we had learned to do in *Theta*. It made all the difference. Tony found that he could now hold her on her course and she was going like a train. Seven hours later I swung back aboard as we nosed into Plymouth Harbour, to tie up among all the big ocean racers moored there in preparation for the race. We were on time.

I dashed ashore and caught the last train back to London to work, as my holiday did not start until the following week. I left Tony to go over all the rigging and gear and generally get her ready to go to Spain.

Coming back the following Friday night, I found *Sopranino* all ready to go. Tony had shifted her to a more sheltered spot and now she was lying just astern of Captain Illingworth's yacht, the *Myth of Malham*. I went over to have a word with him; apparently he had been for a sail in *Sopranino* with Tony and found her rather light and tender. I asked him about the race. He looked at me for a moment.

'You'll do it', he said. That was enough.

Next morning was the day of the race. It was blowing hard from the southwest with driving rain and the weather forecast was not encouraging. Aboard the big racers there was a frenzy of activity as their crews prepared them for heavy weather. We were lying alongside one of the larger boats, busily packing our own stores below, when one of her crew paused in passing to look down at the tiny piece of nonsense preparing to go to sea in that weather, and called down: 'Where are *you* bound?'

We mentioned Santander as casually as we could. He laughed at our little joke and went about his business.

To avoid congestion at the starting line the smaller ocean

The Die is Cast

racers were to start at 10.45, while the larger ones were to start at 11.00. At 10.30 Captain Illingworth came over in his dinghy and said: 'Are you ready?'

'Yes', we replied.

'Fine. Off you go, then.'

We slipped our lines and slid away from the dock, out towards the unfriendly sea. We were in this thing now, for better or for worse.

Out in Plymouth Sound some of the big boys were already milling around, tuning up for the start. As we came out one of them nosed up to us, like a Great Dane shooing away an impudent Pekingese, then swung round to hiss past us, waving a friendly farewell.

Outside, in the Channel, the weather was being rather beastly, blowing hard from the southwest, dead against us, while the driving rain was cutting down the visibility so that the coast on each side of us rapidly dropped away out of sight.

Soon the big boys came out and rapidly overhauled us, charging by in great bounds, their keels coming half out of the water as they leaped over the waves. An hour or so later they had all disappeared out of sight ahead and we were alone once more.

All that day and all that night we banged and bounced our way into the storm, and then on Sunday afternoon as we closed the French coast we made out two other sails. We dived for the binoculars, to peer at them. They were two of the big ocean racers, behind us after 32 hours to windward. Little boats could go to windward in storms.

Tony came off watch as we rounded Ushant Island, and *Sopranino's* nose pointed out across the wide Bay of Biscay. He paused in the hatch as he went below: 'Well?'

'Yes', I said. He turned in and fell fast asleep.

For the next three days and night we sailed straight on to the south, towards Spain. It was a thrill to come up out of the tiny cabin in the middle of the night to find her racing across the seas, reefed down and heeling over so that the helmsman had to sit right out on the side to hold her up, and then take

Sopranino

over and reel off a few more miles towards Santander. It was only the second time we had sailed *Sopranino* and we were now a hundred miles from any land. She was having a good work-out.

I reckoned that on Thursday morning we should see the high mountains that lie back from the Spanish coast and, as the sun came up, there they were. A few hours later we were closing in with a strong westerly wind pushing up great rolling seas. We made out the entrance to the harbour dead ahead, though we only got a glimpse of the coast as we came to the top of each wave before we plunged down into the hollows again, where even the mountain tops were lost to view.

Rounding the headland we hoisted our great big Red Ensign and our quarantine flag, and worked our way across to where the fleet of some thirty-four ocean racers were anchored off the magnificent Yacht Club, a vast building as big as a block of flats out over the water. Its three long rows of balconies were crowded with all the social set from Madrid who had come down for the event.

It was mid-day, calm and sunny in the harbour, and the crews of all the big yachts were on deck, relaxing and enjoying a drink after their strenuous passage from England. As we sailed in through them a cheer went up, first from one boat and then from another until it was all around the fleet and had spread to the crowds on the balconies of the Yacht Club itself.

We looked around to see what it was all about. And then the awful truth dawned on us that they were all looking at us. We didn't know whether to raise our hats politely or pretend we hadn't noticed.

Fortunately the committee launch came chugging out to lay us a mooring anchor, and soon we were sitting down to a fine meal and a bottle of wine on the Club balcony, while Morin Scott, the well-known sailor and author, kindly tidied up aboard *Sopranino* for us.

The race had started on Saturday morning. The first of the big boats had arrived at Santander on Wednesday morning and they had kept on coming in, in ones and twos, all through

The Die is Cast

Wednesday afternoon and night, the last ones arriving on Thursday morning. These were the ocean racing fleet, the cream of the big deep-sea yachts. And little *Sopranino* had turned up only a few hours later.

Recognition at last. To be truthful, our arrival in Santander could not have been better timed if we had staged it. In a few minutes Captain Illingworth, who had been encouraging us quietly all along, came over: 'Excellent, Patrick'.

And then a cable from Laurent Giles: 'WELL SAILED SOPRAN-INO'.

We felt that we had won Round One, on points, at least.

A few days later we sailed our leisurely way back across the Bay of Biscay, stopping this time at La Rochelle and the Ile d'Yeu, slipping through the dangerous Chenal du Four where the tide runs at 10 knots, causing lighthouses to throw up wakes like destroyers as the water rushes past them, back into the English Channel.

Running down Channel towards our home port of Lymington, we were favoured by a nice gale from astern. I hung on to all sail to see what would happen, until Tony called out to me in the middle of the night and said: 'Can't we stop this mad motorboating?'

It was magnificent. The gale had hardened a little and now we were planing, skimming over the top of the water the way a speedboat does, bouncing from wave to wave in the inky darkness and throwing up great sheets of spray. A few of the lighter racing yachts will surf-ride on the face of a wave, but planing is strictly for speedboats and racing dinghies. And there we were in our comfortable cabin boat, streaking along in the dark like a seaplane at take-off.

However, we *were* at least forty miles offshore and you *could* run into things in the dark, so we reduced sail and went on in a more ladylike fashion.

Next morning the Isle of Wight loomed up ahead and a few hours later we were in Lymington, handing out tunny that we had caught in the Bay of Biscay two days before. We had completed over twelve hundred miles in our three weeks' cruise

Sopranino

to Spain and France, and arrived home exactly twenty minutes behind schedule. A good start.

That winter a small band of enthusiasts met at the Royal Ocean Racing Club under the presidency of Captain Illingworth, to form a club to promote the development of this new breed of midget offshore racing boats. We called it the Junior Offshore Group, which shortens nicely to JOG, and drew up a set of rules intended primarily to ensure the highest possible standard of safety. We could not afford to risk an accident, especially at that early stage.

Two more sisters to *Sopranino* were built, while several further boats on similar lines were designed or projected, but they were slow in coming out. Meanwhile the skeleton fleet set out in the spring of 1951 to sail a series of week-end races totalling a thousand miles in the short season.

We had our problems in those early days, but it turned out to be immense fun, racing together across the Channel to France on a Friday night, spending Saturday in a foreign country, and racing home on Sunday.

And more important, we were proving time and time again that not one but several of these miniature craft could go out on to the open sea in all weathers and come safely home on time.

Still there were those who doubted, those who sat at home and muttered: 'It isn't safe. Some day somebody will get killed, you mark my words.' All of us who sailed in these little boats were more and more sure that they were as safe as anything else that sailed the sea, if not safer; but you could not convince the diehards. They just would not believe it was possible.

I don't quite know when the idea came to me, but the more the opponents of these tiny craft spoke up against them the more I felt it was imperative to do something about it. And all through that summer it kept coming back, the idea of sailing *Sopranino* across the Atlantic Ocean to America to show the world just what she *would* do. And slowly it grew and grew.

I myself felt sure that it was possible, if we tackled it the right way. The point was, what was it worth? Was it worth giving up a very good and safe job for, and maybe risking one's life and that of one's crew for many months on the broad Atlantic? That was the question.

Perhaps it was inevitable that one day I should wake up and say to myself: 'We'll have a go'. I had made my decision. The die was cast.

CHAPTER THREE

Building Up

Colin Agrees to Come—The Expedition Is Kept a Secret—Modifications—Division of Responsibility—Routes and Timings—Trade Winds and Hurricanes—Doctors and Dentists—The Fish Man—Patrick Lands in Jail—Falmouth—The Last Base— Hannibal Comes Aboard—We Sail Away from England

FﾁsT things first. Above and beyond all else there was one factor on which the whole expedition would hinge when the time came: the crew. When it comes to a showdown it is the men who fail, not the boats, and for an extreme test of this kind only the best will do. *Sopranino* only carries two men, so either of them must be fully capable of taking charge of her in any conditions if the other should be injured or fall sick.

It was also important that whoever went with me should be able to fill the gaps in my own capabilities. Maintaining the ship and her gear in first-class condition throughout the voyage would obviously be vital. Unfortunately, if I try to knock a nail into a piece of wood the nail bends over, the wood splits, and the head flies off the hammer and drops into the sea. So an ability to handle tools was essential in my crew.

But more important still, he would have to have the temperament and training, coupled with a real love and understanding of the sea, that would keep him going through the many arduous months ahead. There were perhaps a dozen men in England qualified for the job and of those, three or four might be available. After long and careful consideration I settled on Colin Mudie as my first choice, and decided to approach him first.

He was a well-known skipper at the age of twenty-six, to whom I had often lent *Sopranino* for JOG races while I helped out other owners. He was a good navigator and had served his

Building Up

time in a yard as a boatbuilder, so that he would be fully capable of tackling any repairs that might be necessary, either at sea or in remote foreign ports.

As Laurent Giles's Blue-Eyed Boy he had been responsible for the detail drawings of *Sopranino*. He had grown very fond of the little boat and was firmly convinced of her outstanding ability as a sea boat. So one Friday evening I rang him up and said I was coming down to Lymington. Would he care to have dinner with me? He would.

As I put the receiver down after Patrick's call I remember turning to a fellow draughtsman beside me to say:

*'Wonder what the man is up to this time. Either a bigger and better headsail or else he is off across the Atlantic.'**

That evening we had a good dinner and a bottle of wine, discussing generalities. Finally I said, quite casually, 'I have decided to sail *Sopranino* across the Atlantic Ocean to America. Will you come?'

He looked at me for a moment. 'Yes.'

And that was the end of *that* conversation.

Immediately we got down to the details. I had decided to cross by the southern route, in the trade winds, so the best time to make the actual passage would be in December or January, after the hurricane season was finished. On the other hand it was important for us to get away from England by the end of August at the latest, before the September gales started in the Channel.

We both wanted to sail in the big ocean racers in the Fastnet Race, the principal event that year. This would take about four days around August 10, so the immediate idea was for us to get *Sopranino* ready for the long voyage and sail her to Falmouth, where we would make our advanced base; then we could go off for the race, to return to Falmouth and sail as soon as possible afterwards.

The next morning, Saturday, we drove over to see a mutual

*Colin's remarks and comments throughout will appear in italics to distinguish them from my narrative.

Sopranino

friend, Michael Henderson, who was then working at a yacht yard in nearby Hamble. We told him of our plans and he agreed to help us with the preparation, on the understanding that if one of us should fall sick at the last moment he should have his berth.

Mike was so keen to go that though I did sympathise with him, I took care not to stand too close to him on the decks of boats and on stagings, and always swapped my drink for his.

From the start we kept the whole thing secret, telling only our parents and closest friends of our intentions. Far too many such expeditions had started off in a blaze of advance publicity and then got nowhere. We told our various friends in the yachting press exactly what we intended to do, but asked them not to release the news until we had at least reached Spain and achieved something. This they all agreed to do.

Sopranino had just returned from the JOG race to Ostend and was in Dover. The first thing, then, was for me to go down there to fetch her to Hamble for a refit, while Colin drew up plans for certain modifications for the long voyage.

None of my immediate sailing friends was available to come with me. However, through Morin Scott, whom I had met in Santander the year before, I was introduced to John Noakes, who joined me in Dover the next weekend. Thus one more link was forged in a curious chain of circumstances that was to result in our getting a base at Falmouth and Mike Henderson's getting a wife.

As we left the inner basin of Dover Harbour the man on the lock gate called out: 'You will be crossing the Atlantic in that thing next'.

We laughed politely and faded out into the lowering dusk.

On the way down Channel, John mentioned that his mother lived in Falmouth and suggested that we might stay with her while we were getting ready to leave. So it came about that our advanced base was organised.

At Hamble, Mike and Colin took charge of the boat, organising all the thousand and one details of getting her in perfect trim. There were two major modifications to be made. The

Building Up

first was to install a slightly shorter mast. This was necessary since it was not possible to climb up to the top of the tall racing mast without tipping the boat over. In the Channel it would be possible to let the boat go over on her side and then do any repairs while swimming in the water beside her. But where we were going there would be sharks, and the idea somehow seemed less attractive. With the shorter mast we would be able to go up and inspect it, or even do odd jobs up there at sea in some comfort.

The other modification was the addition of an aluminium rail about a foot high around the after part of the deck. This was partly to prevent us from falling off, but more to prevent us from trailing a careless hand over the side and having it nipped off by a passing shark.

While all this was going on I returned to London to get down to the administrative details. Right from the start we had agreed on a clear division of responsibility. Colin was responsible for all matters of maintenance of the ship, while I would look after the general planning and running of the expedition, together with all administrative details.

First I went to the Royal Geographical Society, to see their meteorological expert. We discussed the winds of the world and the ocean currents. Our best route lay *via* Spain and Portugal to Africa and the Canary Islands, thence across the ocean to the West Indies and through the chain of islands to the United States.

That way our longest individual passage would be the 2,700 sea miles (just over 3,000 land miles) from the Canaries to the West Indies. Providing food and water for that passage would be one of the limiting factors in the whole operation.

In addition to the southwesterly gales which might be quite fierce in the Bay of Biscay and down the Portuguese coast, we would have to look out for the chance hurricane that might appear at any time, though it was unlikely that we should meet one much before June.

Then, off Cuba, there would be waterspouts, lightning showers, and tropical revolving storms—sort of baby hurricanes lasting maybe an hour or so but quite powerful while they lasted.

I went back to my warm cosy flat and considered these things, trying to work out in advance all the disasters that could possibly happen and provide as far as possible the right equipment to meet them. After that they would have to be accepted as part of the calculated risk that one must expect to take on an expedition of this kind.

We each went to our own dentists for a check-up. Toothache a thousand miles from land was not a happy thought. I had read somewhere of an experienced ocean voyager who had all his teeth pulled out before he started. It seemed a fine simple solution to the problem, but a little extreme, so we let that one go.

Consider living on Ryvita and apples without teeth. Firmly declined that suggestion.

At the doctor's I went into the question of what to do about a severe appendix case, and was assured that so long as we followed the rules he prescribed it would not be necessary for us to have our appendixes out beforehand. Apparently you lay the boy down in his bunk, keep him warm and still, and feed him on milk only. Like this, he stands a good chance of lasting up to a fortnight, which seemed fair enough, so I added a few extra cans of milk to the stores list and left it at that.

For the rest, we assembled a large bag of assorted medical stores and a good book on how to use them, plus a fair amount of miscellaneous advice.

My next visit was to the Royal Zoological Society, to see the fish man and inquire what he had in his ocean. He was a cheerful soul who warmly assured me that it was full of the most surprising things.

There would of course be sharks that could bite through our frail craft with the greatest ease if it should occur to them. The thing was not to tantalise them by spilling blood overboard or allowing our shadows to fall on the water. I assured him we would not upset them so.

Patrick worked out a drill for encountering sharks which met these

Building Up

requirements admirably. When a dorsal fin was sighted, the man on watch jumped down the hatch and firmly into his bunk, from which point of vantage he woke the other by shouting: 'Your watch!'

There would be whip sharks that could smash our boat in with a single blow of their powerful tails. The trick with them was they always sounded, or dived, before striking, so the drill there was to watch for them to sound and then steer *over* them. That would fool them every time, he said. I hoped he was right.

Down in the Gulf of Paria, off Trinidad, we might find the odd anaconda, a species of water python only much bigger, that sometimes ran as much as fifty feet long and could swallow a man whole. These should be shot in the eye, if we could persuade them to stay still while we did it.

Then he went on to talk about a species of giant octopus that lives in the deep ocean and sometimes comes up on to the surface at night.

'How big?' he said. 'Well, they rarely exceed eighty feet across, though they have been known to grapple with ships' boats and of course they can drag a fully grown whale to the bottom.'

'Of course', I agreed.

'How to tackle them? Well, the accepted method is to turn them inside out and bite them between the eyes.'

I thanked him politely and went home to cook myself a nice fish dinner. If we were going to play this game I might as well get my shot in first.

Meanwhile Colin and Mike had been forging ahead with the preparation of the boat. She was back in the water again, her bottom painted and most of the work done, though several small items had not come through yet and the guard rail was not ready.

It is one of those things about life that, no matter how long and how carefully you prepare, there will always be certain things that are not ready when the times comes and you will either have to go without or accept substitutes. But now we must move on to Falmouth, where the rest would have to be done.

Sopranino

A JOG race from Lymington to Cherbourg was scheduled just before the Fastnet, so we decided to enter *Sopranino* in that, sailing on to Falmouth afterwards. She would not stand much chance in the race, with her shorter mast and reduced rig, but she had already taken more than her share of the prizes that season.

Colin and Mike were to sail her this time, as far as Cherbourg, while I went along in another boat whose owner had never taken her out to sea before. At dawn the first day out, while I was asleep, the owner decided that it was too rough for his converted whaler, turned her round, and took her back to England.

Mike was due to come back from Cherbourg in another boat, which would leave Colin stranded there with my passport and all my gear while I was still in England. I could not get into France without my passport, so I took the night boat to Jersey, to see what I could do about it.

Arriving there in the early dawn I was immediately placed under arrest for not having a passport, though the island was a British possession. The Fastnet Race was due in a week, and we had both promised to crew in various boats in it. It was no time for me to sit and admire the sunlight from behind bars.

I knew that the French authorities would take a much more lenient view of the whole matter, so after a bit of scratching around I persuaded a local boy who had a light aircraft to run me across to Cherbourg. There I explained my position to the customs officer at the tiny private airfield. He was most helpful and promptly ran me down to the docks in his car. Unfortunately he had to rush off right then as his wife had his dinner ready, but later in the afternoon he came down, took a quick look at my passport, and assured me that everything was now in order. We had a couple of glasses of good French wine and that was that. Wonderful people, the French.

We in Sopranino *had our own piece of fun on the way to Cherbourg. The race was to be started by the committee boat outside the river and she started off first with most of the fleet in tow. The whaler, with* Sopranino *alongside, followed under motor.*

Building Up

Mike and I had just finished fixing the new sails which had only arrived that evening, when the whaler's motor conked out. We let go at once, wishing them good night, and set off to find our way down river in a pitch-black night. Outside we could find no trace of the rest of the fleet until a flashing of searchlights at some distance gave us the idea that the race had started.

We sailed over to the Isle of Wight shore, where we would get the full three- to four-knot tide to take us out to sea. As we came up towards the light of one of the buoys, quite close in the darkness a voice remarked conversationally: 'Hullo, where are you going?'

A little surprised, for we could see nothing but the flashing light on the buoy and it was now after midnight, we replied to the darkness: 'Oh, just off to Cherbourg. The race, you know . . . Er, where are you?'

'On the buoy. Don't stop, but do tell someone that we are here.'

The tide shot us past the buoy and there was no chance of sailing back against it, so we ran inshore to the slack water and sailed up until we thought that we could again reach the buoy. As we got closer, two large steamers arrived and shone searchlights on the scene. One of them anchored and began to lower a boat. The other spotted ourselves and steamed over to talk to us. He dropped us a line and towed us at well above our theoretical maximum speed towards the buoy. Meanwhile the bang of the maroons was calling out the Yarmouth lifeboat and lights were going on all over the town.

As we rushed towards the buoy, perilously attached to the steamer by a bar-taut towing line, we saw in the searchlights that it had a crew of no less than four people, and that there was also a capsized dinghy tied to it. They waved us away when we got close, and told us that thank you very much but they would much rather be rescued by a large and comfortable steamer.

Next day, when we arrived in Cherbourg two hours behind the fleet, no one would believe us.

Two days later we were in Falmouth, where Mike joined us for the final preparations. Then Colin and I had to rush off for the Fastnet Race, which turned out to be a complete frost as far as we were concerned. There was a gale at the start and several of the big boats, including both those in which we were sailing, had to retire within the first few hours due to failure of their gear. I always said big boats weren't safe.

After the race, Colin joined Mike at Falmouth, while I went back to London to settle the final administrative details: wills, powers of attorney, and the like, plus the last-minute stores and equipment.

I said good-bye to my parents and friends, whom I would not be seeing for a long time, assured Colin's father that all was well, we wouldn't set out across the Atlantic unless it was a fine day (what more can you promise?); then down to Falmouth for the last time. A quiet party there, and next morning the car went back home, taking Mike and John Noakes's sister Pat, who had come to see us off.

Falmouth Harbour is one of the most beautiful in England and, on a fine day, perhaps the most beautiful that I have seen anywhere in the world. Steep wooded hills come right down to the shore, while across from the port of Falmouth itself lie the picturesque villages of St Mawes and Flushing. Each of these is a cluster of houses set into the steep hillside of its own headland, with narrow winding roads leading down to the water where an ancient but indomitable ferry boat will take you into the town to do your shopping.

It was in Flushing that Mrs Noakes lived and under her hospitable roof that we stayed, while we put the finishing touches to the boat and loaded her up with the fantastic amount of stores and gear that we should need to last us through more than a year's wandering across the wide Atlantic.

An indication of the style of the establishment aboard Sopranino. *We counted up one day in the West Indies to find that we had twenty-one pairs of trousers on board and seven hats. Patrick and I could not agree about dish mops so we each had our own and that made seven of those. We had notepaper and string and ink and luggage labels. Engineers' vices, saws, chisels and cutlasses and paint, and in fact everything. A friend who was thinking of doing a similar thing asked for a list of the things that we thought he ought to have on board and was somewhat surprised to get a list of 297 different things.*

After confiding our mission to the customs officer in Falmouth, we were allowed to purchase ship's stores of food and the like. Literally hundreds of cans and boxes of all shapes and sizes, for each one of which we had to find a place somewhere in the boat.

I had based my calculations on the assumption that we were going to use all the available space. And I mean *all*. Imagine for a moment that you are setting out to fill up a small room with hundreds of miscellaneous items of all shapes and sizes, not leaving an inch to spare at the ceiling nor wasting an inch behind or under the furniture, and yet you must so pack it that any single item is available at a moment's notice. Quite a job.

At long last all was ready, the last chart checked and the last can stowed away. *Sopranino* was lying deep in the water. Deeper than her designer had ever meant her to. But we stepped aboard and she was still riding the little wavelets in the harbour nicely. When you are used to a boat you can feel when she is unhappy, and *Sopranino* wasn't. She was muttering quietly to herself about all this nonsense that I was asking her to carry, and I suspect that Colin was on her side, but they both accepted the whole thing with a good heart, so we towed her across to the Falmouth side of the harbour and began settling in aboard.

Summer left Falmouth and departed to the south about two weeks before we left. The final coat of paint had perforce to be put on in the damp and we fought that paint for the rest of the voyage. To keep her up to standard we had to paint her topsides every two months or so, whereas if the paint had been properly applied at first it should have lasted most of the way.

Summer we chased down to Spain and caught up with there for three days. We caught up with it again for a week at Lisbon before it got away, and then for a single day at Casablanca. Not until we arrived in the tropics did we really effectively catch up the summer we had in mind.

In the confusion I had almost forgotten Hannibal. Hannibal is an elephant, about four inches long and bright pink. He has his own oilskin jacket and trousers and hat, his personal life-line in case he should fall overboard, a towel around his neck to keep the drips out, and his own hammock which he keeps slung in the radio loop.

Sopranino

A small elephant is absolutely essential aboard a small boat. A large one wouldn't fit. Besides, he has an elephantine thirst. If you are ever lost at sea, you only have to hold him up by his life-line and his trunk will point straight towards the nearest drink.

Now he was swinging quietly in his hammock, gazing at us and wondering what the devil we were up to. That made three of us. Meanwhile we struggled with the immediate problem of creating some semblance of order out of the chaos below.

For those technically interested in hammocks for pink elephants I may say that Hannibal's had five properly spaced holes. He would take the weight off his mind by lying on his tummy with his legs and trunk dangling through the holes. He said he felt more dignified this way up but it may have been the position of our wine locker, which happened to be immediately under his hammock.

Soon it was dark, so we had supper and turned in for a good night's sleep, riding quietly to a mooring out in the harbour, while outside a gentle rain pattered down on the decks and little ripples chuckled along the sides of the ship a few inches from our ears.

In the morning the sky was overcast, with thick low clouds completely cutting out the sun. And underneath it was calm and still. The weather forecast was good, but there was no point in leaving our mooring, since without a motor we should only have drifted helplessly around the harbour.

At lunch time we got a lift ashore in a passing launch, to take a walk around and top up our water supply. Then back aboard again. Still no wind, so there we sat. Soon after dark some friends came over and invited us ashore to their hotel for supper, which invitation we gladly accepted.

Later in the evening, as we were sitting in the hotel wondering whether or not to make a night start, we heard a loud bang and a long screeching whistle, just like a shell being fired from a gun. We went out on to the lawn which overlooks the entrance to the harbour, to find that the local coast defences were having firing practice. The sky was full of red streaks as the tracer shells went bouncing across the water. It was definitely not a good time to be drifting around out there in a small boat, so back aboard we went and into our bunks for the night.

The next morning, Thursday, September 6, it was warm and sunny, with a light northwesterly wind and a good weather forecast. A quick dash ashore to telephone that we were leaving, then we let go our mooring, hoisted sail and drifted slowly across the harbour, washing and shaving and having breakfast as we went.

As far as any passers-by were concerned we were just one more little boat off for a nice sail around the bay. They might have been a little surprised to notice the customs officer come out to wave us a friendly good-bye, for he was one of the few who shared the secret of our immediate destination, Lisbon.

The wind remained light and the sea remained calm as we drifted out of the entrance and past the dangerous Manacles, busily cleaning and stowing, filling the cooking stoves, and adjusting the rigging.

By five in the evening the Lizard was abeam, and we were laying our course for Spain. We were away.

CHAPTER FOUR

Southward Ho!

The Smallest Ship in the World—The Bay of Biscay—Calms and Gales—Corunna and El Ferrol—Gale down the Portuguese Coast—The Gingerbread Castle—We Are Guarded—Cabbages and Kings—Cleaning and Painting—Ceremonial Departure—In and Out of the Tagus

As the sun went down we turned to take a last look at the English coast, green and gold in the sunset. Already the Lizard lighthouse was flashing away on the headland, getting ready for its night's work of guiding ships up and down the Channel. The log was reading 1. One mile covered and perhaps nine thousand to go. For a moment we sat and looked. Perhaps one day, one year, we should see that coast again. Perhaps.

But we had work to do. The wind was in the north behind us, driving *Sopranino* steadily southward towards Spain at four or five knots. If it kept up like that, we should make a hundred miles a day; good going for a little ship.

And she *was* a little ship. When we were getting ready to leave I had persuaded the Board of Trade to register her as a British Merchant Ship. She had already proved that she was well capable of going to sea and it would help when we visited foreign ports. We were carrying a complete set of ship's papers, the same as any great ocean liner. Less than twenty feet long, she was probably the smallest ship in the world.

As the sun dipped to the horizon we hauled down our Red Ensign, furled it, and put it away until we should enter our next port. But between us and our next landfall there lay over four hundred miles of open sea.

After asserting our dignity as a British Ship, the Ensign's secondary function in life was to stop the plastic crockery from jumping out of its rack.

The last time we had crossed the Bay of Biscay we had swung

46

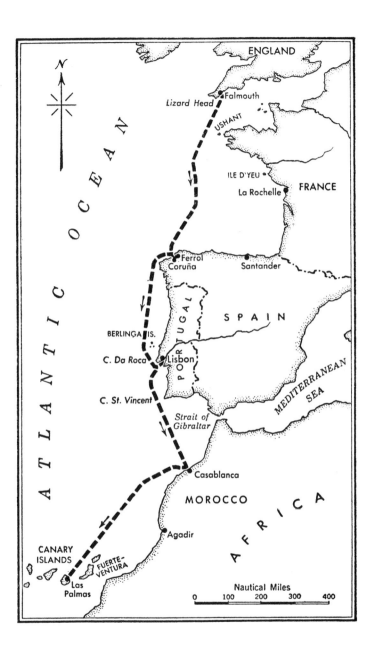

Sopranino

around the western end of France to sail south to Santander. This time it would not be so easy, for we were making for Corunna, in the northwest corner of Spain, and our course lay to the southwest all the way, dead against the prevailing winds.

Last time we had come this way had been in August. We had had a small storm, but nothing serious. This time it was already early September and we could expect the powerful equinoctial gales to strike at any instant.

For the moment the weather forecast was good: moderate northeast winds; some morning fog. We made ourselves some supper of stew and stewed apples and checked the chronometer against the time signals on the radio.

Basic Stew Mark I. The beginning of the end.

Just before midnight the Lizard light dipped and was gone. We were on our own now. Might as well start taking watches. On our previous runs we had worked out a system of watches, designed to insure that each man got his full eight hours' sleep a day.

One of us would take charge of the ship completely, while the other would go below. As soon as his head hit the pillow, the man on watch would note the time by the cabin clock and give him exactly four hours' sleep. Then he would call him, and he would get up, cook a meal, serve it and wash up, do any odd jobs that might be necessary, then dress up in his oilskins and come on deck to take over.

Exactly four hours' sleep it was. Our timepiece was a chronometer and no slackness was encouraged from either end.

Thus, there were no fixed hours, but in fact each man would get four hours' clear sleep twice a day, with variations, so that over a period of days he would find that he was on duty at different times.

Probably the most miserable time is between midnight and four in the morning, the early dawn time when all the world is cold and grey and bleak. Once the sun is up and it is fully light, life gets more cheerful. You begin to feel warm and hopeful and have grandiose thoughts about breakfast, even though you know full well it'll be porridge again.

48

Southward Ho!

During that first night we sailed through the middle of a fishing fleet. It is very cheerful and pleasant to be surrounded by gay little lights bobbing around on the water. Very snug and safe and homely. Past the fishery protection vessel, lying to her anchor in a blaze of lights of all colours, we ran out of the fleet and across a shipping lane.

We always try to get out of the way of the big fellows as fast as we can, especially at night, but this time there were two of them bearing down on us from opposite directions. It is not nice to think of being run over on the high seas by something as big as a block of buildings, so we switched on our white mast-head light and shone our powerful lantern on the white sails. Immediately they both changed course and went off in totally different directions. I sometimes wonder where they fetched up.

By Saturday morning we had made about 120 miles, and then the wind left us, becalmed and rolling in the Atlantic swells some fifty miles off Ushant. Then down came the fog, and for two whole days we sat, while steamers, huge and grey and ghostly, honked their way past us.

To be becalmed in fog near a shipping lane in a small boat is one of life's more trying things. All the time there are fog-horns blaring mournfully away all around you, seeming to come from every direction. Then suddenly you tense as you hear the steady beat of a ship's engines coming closer—and perhaps the splash of her propellers, if she is light.

You know that she cannot possibly see you, though her lookouts may be up in her bows, straining to make out the shapes of other ships in the fog. You know that in a tiny wooden boat, low in the water, you do not even show up on her radar screen. She has no hope of seeing you until it is far too late to change course to miss you.

And without wind you cannot move to avoid her. You just lie there helpless and hope that she will miss you. Each time one came close we would blow our own squeaky little foghorn and sometimes we would hear the clanging of her telegraphs and her engines would stop, as she glided past quite close yet still invisible and ominous.

Sopranino

Then suddenly, about midday on Monday, it lifted and we lay on the smooth calm sea in brilliant sunshine. All at once the steamers became gay friendly things, going about their business with a friendly wave for the little boat out there so far from land.

We decided that we ought to keep ourselves fit by taking exercise. So we organised a Sports Day. One event only—Round the Ship Outside Everything. At the word 'Go' from the man with the stop-watch you leapt out of the cockpit, ducked under the boom, swung around the rigging, two steps forward to round the jib, back outside the rigging on the other side, and around the stern to your seat again at the tiller. Patrick has the record for the course at thirty-seven seconds, but Hannibal maintains that it should be a handicap event.

It was wonderful to be able to bring all our damp things up from the cabin and lay them out in the sun to dry, while we basked in the warmth and admired the ships going by. But already the next piece of nonsense was cooking up. The same evening the weather forecast came in over the radio:

'Deep depression over the Atlantic . . . approaching the British Isles.' Here comes our first gale.

All next day we drifted slowly southward in light airs, while the smooth oily swell from the southwest mounted up and up and the sky clouded over.

On Tuesday evening we huddled around the radio:

'And here is the Shipping Forecast: Gale warning. There will be gales in the areas Shannon, Malin . . .'

It was going to miss us and hit Ireland. Good! Fried onion omelette for supper!

But our joy was short-lived. By midnight there was a smart breeze from the southwest and a moderate sea running. We were beginning to regret those fried onions. Steadily the wind increased in force, building up the seas until by nine in the evening it was too much for her, even with the reduced rig. I had to call Colin out to reef the mainsail and set the storm jib.

Half an hour later we had to heave to, with the wind still rising all the time. By ten it was blowing a full gale, whipping the tops off the seas and howling in the rigging like a wild banshee in the dark. We crawled out on deck, removed every stitch of canvas from her, lashed the helm down, and left her wallowing beam-on to the seas.

For a while we sat below, listening to the storm raging outside, tensing as each big wave hit her and broke thundering over her in a smother of foam. Then we realised that *Sopranino* was, as always, behaving herself like a lady. She was so light that she was climbing right up the waves, just taking the tops of the crests over her, and when anything big did catch her unawares she was giving and going with it without any harm.

We looked at Hannibal, fast asleep in his hammock. Obviously a sensible and intelligent elephant. There was nothing else to be done on deck and we could not hope to make any progress against this weather until it eased off a little, so we might as well do the same. Into our pyjamas, then, and both into our bunks for a nice night's sleep.

In the morning the gale was still doing its stuff nicely. It was hard to believe that not long ago it had been so calm and quiet that when Colin had been asleep I could hear the chronometer ticking away inside its box. Now everything was making a noise. Each little piece of rope or canvas was banging and flapping in a different key, while over it all rose the howl of the wind and the thundering roar of breaking seas.

In the cabin the motion was mostly vertical. Up, up, up she would rise on a wave. Then there would be a little sideways jerk and a crash as the crest broke over her and swept across her decks; then down she would drop, so fast you felt that you were going to rise out of your bunk. A little pause at the bottom, and up she would go again. And so it went on, hour after hour.

At seven o'clock we turned on the radio for the weather forecast. 'Severe gales in the Bay of Biscay.' They were telling *us*! Then of course it dawned on us: all the weather in those parts comes from the southwest, across the Atlantic Ocean. We had run out of the range of the English forecasts and were getting it before the forecasters could forecast it. We didn't speak any Spanish, so we should have to be our own meteorologists from now on.

Sopranino

By eleven in the morning the noise of the wind in the rigging had gone down from a high scream to a steady whine. The gale was easing off. I peered over the side of my bunk and gazed with distaste at a gallon or so of water swooshing from side to side on the floor, swilling four waterlogged shoes to and fro over four sodden socks. Porridge was dripping quietly from the ceiling, and framed in the small opening under the hatch the lead-grey sky was whirling in great arcs.

I recoiled into my bunk and lay on my back pretending to be asleep and hoping that nature would call Colin on deck. No luck. Out of the corner of my half-closed eye I could see that he was doing the same. Heigh-ho. Up Skipper, and do something about it. I eased myself into a sitting position, steadied myself as a wave of nausea swept over me, found the sponge, and started mopping up the mess.

Outside, the cockpit was half full of water. We had left the draincock closed, so the rest must have been shaken out. By the time I had tidied that up Colin was dressed. He was less fortunate than I and usually felt rather more seasick at times like this. However, out he came, and together we hoisted the reefed mainsail and jib.

I estimated that while we had been lying to we had drifted back about twelve miles. Now to make it up. Off we went, rising and dipping over the waves, climbing up to windward again.

By supper time I was feeling a lot better and ventured below to tidy up and cook some hot porridge. That was much better. The wind had eased still further so, full of hot food and bravado, we shook out our reef and pounded on to the southward.

All next day, Friday, it continued to blow good and hard. One of us would go on deck, tear off twenty miles to windward, then heave her to and come below, radiating smugness, to cook some more hot food. Then the other would try his hand, and so on.

Judging by the number of ships around we must have run on to one of the shipping lanes, though which one we could not be sure. We had not had a chance for a shot at the sun for a couple of days, while we had been drifting around on all sorts of different courses, and the signals from the Spanish radio beacons were coming in too faintly to be any real good.

Towards midnight the gale began to hot up again, so we turned off to the eastward and went scooting off the shipping lane before taking down our sails and lying-to once more. This time we were too near the big shipping to risk both sleeping at once, so we took turns standing watch, one sitting in the hatch keeping a look-out while the other slept.

It was lucky that we did, for during Colin's watch several ships came past in the dark. In fact one came straight at us until he flashed the lantern at it, when it changed course to clear us.

By midday the wind had begun to ease again. At the height of the gale the pressure of the wind on the mast and rigging alone had been enough to keep *Sopranino* at a steady angle of heel. But now she began rolling wildly, so out I went on deck to set the sails and heave her to, to steady her while I tidied up below and cooked breakfast.

I woke Colin and served him breakfast in bed, which is a nice civilised thought in a little boat in a gale at sea, but to tell the truth there was not room in the cabin for two people to sit up at once, so that if we were both below one of us had to eat in his bunk.

A small coaster named *Yser* came close past us as we were eating. The waves were really quite large by then, after a couple of days of gale, and although she was quite a sizeable ship and not more than a hundred yards away, when she went down in the troughs she disappeared completely, masts and all. As she came up on a crest, we showed her our Red Ensign. Her skipper waved enthusiastically and pointed ahead of us.

Presumably there was land ahead somewhere. The interesting question was Where? And what land? We had now been nine days out of sight of land, drifting around in calms and being swept all over the place by gales and currents of unknown strength. For several days we had had no chance of a sun sight to fix our position, so precisely where we were was an open question.

If we assumed that my estimated position, after all that drifting around, might be out as much as ten per cent, then the best that we could say was that we were probably somewhere within a circle sixty miles in diameter. We looked up in the pilot book to see what sort of a coast lay ahead. High, steep cliffs and some outlying rocks—just the thing to bump into during a dark night in a gale.

We found out when we arrived there that it is known locally as the Coast of Death.

After we had finished our meal we went up on deck, to find that the wind had eased still further, so we shook out our reef, set the big jib, and laid our course for Corunna. When we had left Falmouth I had hoped that we might be lucky and make Lisbon in one hop, but with the calm and the gale we had taken much longer to cross the Bay of Biscay than we had the last time.

There was no point in straining anything on the first passage, so we decided to put into Corunna to pick up fresh food and water and have a couple of days' rest, before pushing on down to Lisbon.

In the evening I got a fix on the radio. It was still rather nebulous, and you cannot really trust radio bearings that come off a steep coast at an angle, as the beam is likely to bend as it crosses the coast, but it suggested that we were about thirty miles south of our estimated position. This was quite possible, since the log was new and a little stiff and could be reading low.

We were definitely on a shipping lane, which agreed with the radio's story, so we charged on through the darkness towards where we thought Corunna should be, keeping a good look-out ahead. A boat has no headlights, and waving a lantern around doesn't help, so at a time like this you just sit there at the tiller, straining to make out signs of anything that may lie in the darkness ahead.

Wonder of wonders! Next morning the wind moderated to

a nice strong breeze and swung around behind us, driving us easily and comfortably over the waves. The sun shone out of a clear blue sky, drying out all our clothes and bedding as we sat on deck, shaving and primping ourselves for our arrival in Spain. Even Hannibal was out on deck, basking in the sun and gazing with disgust at all those gallons and gallons and gallons of Water.

At midday we got a sight on the sun *and* a bearing on Cabo Villano radio beacon. Now we knew where we were: just about where we thought. We altered course a little to take us clear of Cabo Prior and sailed happily on.

Just after dark a light appeared on the port bow, flashing. Obviously a lighthouse, but which one? The Spanish lights are very confusing. Instead of giving, say, three flashes in a row, they will give two, then pause, and then another one. It would not be so bad from the deck of a ship, where you can see over the waves, but in a little boat you shoot up on to the top of a wave, see a flash, and disappear into the hollows again. The next time you come up you see, maybe, two flashes. Now where are you? It's all very difficult. However, we were reasonably certain where we were, so on we went. And about one in the morning there was the Tower of Hercules that guards the entrance to Corunna Harbour, flashing away clearly ahead of us.

Not having originally planned to call at Corunna, I had no detailed chart of the entrance, so we hove-to to have a sleep until dawn. After breakfast we came on deck to look at the long sweeping panorama of the Spanish coast. High steep cliffs swinging around in a great bay. And there, in the middle, the Tower of Hercules and Corunna.

By two in the afternoon we were sailing past the Tower into the entrance to the harbour, admiring the gay white houses with red roofs piled up on the steep shore. Our huge Red Ensign fluttered proudly in the breeze behind us.

Inside, across the quiet sleepy harbour, we made out the fine large building of the Real Club Nautico de la Coruña. Slowly we drifted across the still calm water, to glide silently to

Sopranino

a stop alongside the Club jetty, eleven days out of Falmouth, some five hundred miles away.

Corunna is a strange harbour. Before the war it had been a busy commercial port, but now the trade had gone elsewhere, leaving the wide docks and quays deserted and silent except for a couple of fishing boats being built high on the shore and one whaling ship lying to her anchor in the middle.

Ashore all was bustle and activity. The town had come into prominence as a seaside resort and new buildings were going up all over the place. But the docks did not share this prosperity. They just lay there, silent in the sunlight, remembering better days.

A few people were swimming from the Yacht Club steps. A couple who spoke English came over to us and politely asked what we wanted. We explained that we had come across the Bay of Biscay from England and would like to rest for a couple of days before going on to Lisbon.

They immediately led us, in our dirty sailing clothes, up through the magnificent lounges and bars of the Club, to have a good meal and a bottle of wine on the balcony. Perhaps we would like to sleep ashore and take a cabin in the Club for the night? We certainly would.

Going up the huge curved staircase I kept falling over. I just could not get back my land legs after so many days of wild motion on the sea. Upstairs we were shown to our cabins. Each was a fine comfortable bedroom with its own bathroom and entrance hall, almost like a small apartment, decorated to look like a ship's cabin, with ships' lamps, and anchors embroidered on the pillows.

We were a little worried by all this luxury. We had left England with about £75 between us, to travel thousands of miles to four continents and many countries. We might pick up a little more money later on, but not much, so we had to be very careful with our pennies. As casually as I could I asked what the charge was per night. Five shillings. What a country!

We put *Sopranino* away in the little basin behind the Club, among all the skiffs and dinghies, and decided to take a holiday

Southward Ho!

and spend a couple of nights ashore. The immigration officer called, but was met by the Secretary of the Club, who assured him that he would look after us, and departed.

We collected our waterproof suitcase, containing our best shore-going clothes, took it up to our rooms, and retired to our bathrooms to enjoy the delight of a real tub. Then down we went, feeling wonderful in our clean clothes, to stroll around the town.

In our sailing clothes we had slunk into this magnificent Yacht Club behind our hosts. After a shower and a shave we roused out our Number One shore-going clothes, with reefer jackets and white pants and all that the complete yachtsman at Cowes could desire, and swept grandly down the main staircase. The doorman took one quick look, wrenched off his hat as he bowed, and opened the doors as wide as they would go—which evened up that one.

Here we discovered the answer to that problem that has been taxing the nautical sages for years. 'Where do speedboats go in their old age?' Answer: To Spain, where they are fitted with high, flaring bulwarks and a little pilot house and a one-lung engine. Now they are almost indistinguishable from the genuine home-built sardine fisher.

Perhaps it was the contrast with the tiring, anxious days before, when for day after endless day we had struggled to gain insignificant distances across the wide Bay of Biscay to Spain, that made it feel so wonderful to be there at last.

Or perhaps it was the feeling that finally, after so many months of preparation, we were on our way and getting somewhere. Or maybe it was just Spain, with its sunshine, its charming, happy, friendly people and its slow, easy-going way of life. Just sitting there under the shady trees, sipping a drink and watching the girls go by, we felt a wonderful sense of contentment and sheer delight in life.

Spanish girls are most exotic, colourful, and gay, but do tend to be a little tubular in section.

We took two whole days off, a week-end in the middle of the week. Ocean voyagers do not live by clocks and calendars, but by the sun and the wind and the way of the sea. In the morning we would swim with the crowd of men and girls in the warm

57

water by the Yacht Club steps. In the afternoon we would stroll through the quiet back streets of the town or take a ride on a tram full of people laughing and singing. They are a happy people. A few of them are very rich. Most of them are very poor. But always they are laughing and gay.

In an ice-cream shop I asked the proprietor for a match. He couldn't find one but he wandered down the street a few doors to borrow some. The shop was full of people waiting to be served, but nobody minded. Nobody was in a hurry and the conversation was good, so why worry? Anything that was not done today could be done tomorrow or the day after.

Presently he came back with a box of matches, smiling proudly, and after we had exchanged a few words with everybody in the shop who could speak a little English and the whole thing had been properly discussed, we went on our way.

In the evening there would be parties and dancing at the Club, and then back to our warm, dry, wide, comfortable, stationary beds for the night. But all good things must come to an end, and after our two days we moved back aboard *Sopranino* to prepare to leave.

We had arrived on Monday afternoon. On Wednesday afternoon we topped up our water supply, bought some fresh food, and moved the boat out into the harbour to anchor for the night, ready to sail away.

That night Colin fell sick of some kind of poisoning. For two days we lay out there in the harbour, rolling to our anchor while the wind steadily increased in force. The next gale was coming up. By the time he was fit again it was Sunday and the wind was blowing good and hard from the west.

It would have been a waste of time to start out for Lisbon in that weather; we should only have worn ourselves out getting nowhere. So we decided to sail across to El Ferrol, the naval harbour that lies about ten miles across the sheltered entrance to the eastward.

El Ferrol Harbour is a natural lake, perhaps five miles long by one mile wide, surrounded by mountains and joined to the sea by a long, narrow neck of water at its northern end. Sailing in in the evening time, we found several small warships and one large cruiser at anchor, and over to the eastern side a small walled harbour, next to the town.

As we ran in past the warships we, as courtesy demands, dipped our ensign. This in Sopranino *involves a mere twitch of the wrist compared with the working party it takes to dip a man-o'-war's ensign, so we were more than gratified when each warship punctiliously replied.*

We ran into this smaller harbour and lay between a buoy and the wall, among fishing boats and sand barges, looking straight across the street at a line of shops. In the morning we were awakened quite early by the noise of people bustling to and fro on the quayside. Men were unloading the barge by hand, carrying sand up to waiting carts a basketful at a time, while more carts came rattling down the street at a full gallop, their drivers standing up and cracking their whips like charioteers.

In the afternoon we caught the little ferry boat to the north side of the harbour, towards the sea. It stopped at an ancient jetty and the passengers wandered through a dark workshop where smiths were busy with their forges, then up a steep winding path on to the little road that led up the side of the mountain to the village.

Patrick had decided that for exercise, after being cooped up in our little boat at sea, we should make a point of climbing the local mountain at every port of call. This we did faithfully, but fortunately the one at El Ferrol was the only one we climbed on foot.

The village itself was strikingly similar to Flushing, in Cornwall, where we had made our last base in England, with its clean white-washed houses and narrow winding street. Above the village we followed the path up the hill and looked out over the Spanish countryside, rolling green and brown, with a little brown village, in a hollow, where a man was mending the church bell and every now and then sending a clear note across the valley.

Up at the top of the hill we stood on a flat rock among the heather, gazing out over the open sea, with Corunna away on the left. Behind us the fleet of warships in the harbour looked like toy boats in a child's bath.

Sopranino

An interesting point about looking at the sea from the top of a hill is the amount of it that you can see at once. It appears incredible that in mere days or even weeks you can make any worthwhile progress across it. On board a small boat it is impossible, at the best of times, to see more than perhaps two miles in any direction, and this only when you rise up on a crest. For most of the time your horizon of water tops and froth is just beside you. Perhaps it is this that keeps the sea from being a lonely place.

Down the steep hillside through the village, we caught the ferry back to El Ferrol. Strolling through the town towards the dock, we ran into an officer of the Spanish Navy to whom we had had an introduction from Corunna. He was in a hurry at that moment as they were busy installing a new Admiral, but he found time to dart into a house, collect eight girls—including the Admiral's daughter—and bundle us off with them to the Tennis Club for the evening.

All that night it rained and blew, but by the following afternoon it began to clear up. However, the weather forecast was still very unfavourable, so we accepted the invitation of our naval officer friend to dine aboard the cruiser *Almirante Cervera*, the largest warship in the Spanish Navy.

In the evening it was calm and clear as we sailed with him across the harbour in *Sopranino* to visit the cruiser. A sailor was detailed to guard *Sopranino* as we went aboard, and we left him holding her like a toy boat alongside the great warship in the white glare of her floodlights.

We left him standing to attention at the top of the gangway with our masthead firmly clutched in one hand. Hannibal, who had not been invited, glared pinkly and distantly from the hatch.

Later we drifted quietly across the harbour to our dock with a couple of bottles of Spanish wine that the officers had insisted we take 'for the galley', and so to bed.

It was not until Thursday, September 27, that the weather finally cleared and we sailed away, bound south for Lisbon. The forecast was still not good and there were signs of wind in the high clouds, but we could not afford to wait any longer, so we went.

Southward Ho!

About twenty miles out the wind left us, becalmed in the pouring rain, heaving on the oily swell, our sails slatting to and fro. All through Friday and Saturday and Sunday we drifted along the Spanish coast, sometimes moving a yard or two, but mostly not, while the sea calmed down until it was as flat as a pancake.

As we rounded Finisterre on a fine glossy blue sea with just an air of wind to keep us moving, I made a note in my log that a large P. & O. liner that was passing near enough for me to read her name was disappearing to her mastheads behind the long swell.

Once or twice we did get a little breeze and would skim along, throwing up a little spray. At one of these times we ran through a great patch of oil left on the water by a steamer who discharged it as she passed us. Somehow we managed to bring it below into the cabin on our oilskins and for days we had the sickly smell of the stuff all around us, until we finally cleaned it all out with detergent.

On Monday a breeze came up and began building up into a strong wind from the northwest, sweeping us around the corner of Spain. By Tuesday it had reached light gale force and swung into the north, behind us, pushing up the sea and driving us scooting down the Portuguese coast at high speed. Sometimes we stayed on the same wave for as much as twelve seconds at a time, heavily laden as we were.

Only once did we get a twelve-second surf, but eights and nines and tens came from every third or fourth wave. It was a most exhilarating business to be thus forging down the coast to Lisbon with great heaps of phosphorescent spray on both sides, apparently solid and moving with us. The wind was dead behind us and steering was tricky. Eventually it became too scarifying and we pulled down and stowed the mainsail. In the last two hours the log had given us fifteen miles. We must have averaged eight knots during the last hour.

Down came the mainsail and on we went to the southward. Soon the wind had risen further and we were planing along in the dark, about forty miles offshore. *Sopranino* was really on the step this time, her bow high out of the water, a great fan of phosphorescent spray shimmering in the darkness on each side

Sopranino

of us, while out behind we left a long blue-white trail on the sea.

The visibility around us was very poor and ahead of us the dangerous Berlengas Islands stretched out some twenty miles from the coast, across our path, just before Lisbon. Time to get to work on the radio direction-finder. That was my job, so down I went into the cabin to lie on my side in my bunk, twiddling dials and counting squeaks, the book of signals in one hand, pencil and paper wedged under my left shoulder, and a whistle between my teeth.

Outside Colin was doing his bronco-busting act at the tiller. Obviously he had no hope of keeping the boat on an exact course while I worked, so he did his best to keep her in the right general direction and each time I got a bearing I would blow my whistle. Then he would quickly read his compass and shout down what course we had actually been on at that time, leaving me to do sums to find out the true bearing I'd taken.

It sounds crazy but it worked. I drew four lines from four radio beacons along the coast and they all crossed within a mile of each other. Now at least we knew where we were.

We were level with the Berlengas Islands and clear of them, though we could not see the lighthouse at all, so we swung around them to come in on a safe bearing towards Cabo Roca lighthouse, by Lisbon. For the rest of the night we rushed on towards the shore, down the radio beam with the gale under our tail. Then, just before dawn, it came flashing through the rain, dead ahead of us. Colin let out a Highland Howl: 'Horoo for the Goon Box'. We were on the beam.

Cabo Roca light appeared dead ahead from the murk and not more than four miles away. The light, in normal weather, is visible for twenty-five miles.

By nine in the morning we were sailing across Cascais Bay, past beautiful Estoril, under the shelter of the land. All along the shore there were low cliffs topped by green fields and trees with gay little houses scattered among them, while down by the water's edge midget-sized electric trains ran busily to and fro.

And lots and lots of little motor cars. At that moment I felt that if there was anything that I did desire in the world it was a ride in a motor car.

Southward Ho!

Going through the narrow North Channel, to enter the Tagus River, we were hailed by a Spanish steamer with a pilot aboard and offered a tow. We smiled, but refused his kind offer. On a voyage like this one dare not accept a tow *into* a harbour. A tow *out* of a harbour is fine, but if you accept one when you are coming in, no matter if it is a flat calm, you may be sure that the next day you will find that according to the local newspapers you have been rescued. And we were not out to prove that little boats needed rescuing.

Half-way up the Tagus to Lisbon we hove to by a cluster of brightly painted fishing boats to dry out and clean up before changing into our best whites for our arrival at the Yacht Club.

Then on up the river, past an incredible little castle, standing alone out on a sandy spit, that looked for all the world as though it was made of gingerbread, and into Lisbon Harbour, our last base in Europe, 300 miles from Corunna and some 800 from England.

As you sail up the Tagus, the river widens out into a sort of vast lake, full of big ships at anchor, swinging to the tide. On your right a range of green hills parallel to the river runs down to marshes, with an occasional sandy beach. Quite deserted; not a house, nothing.

On your left the city of Lisbon is built on a wide low hill, stretching from the palace and fortress at the top down through the shopping and business districts to the docks along the river.

On we sailed, past huge liners and busy tugs, dodging between them and the vast number of large sailing barges that bring cork down the Tagus from the countryside above, looking for the customs house. Then suddenly *they* found *us*.

There was a loud war-whoop from behind and a large tug, all white with the one word '*Police*' on her bows, came charging at us. We dodged her and stopped while she came fussing alongside with a great clanging of bells.

A police officer came out of her wheelhouse and motioned Colin, who was standing on *Sopranino's* foredeck, to come aboard. No sooner had he stepped across than there was more

Sopranino

clanging and she set off at high speed through the maze of shipping, with *Sopranino* in hot pursuit.

Neither Colin nor I speak a single word of Portuguese and, as I followed them in towards the quays, I had visions of feeding him buns through the bars of the local jail, if I were not inside myself.

When at last I caught them they were tied up to the customs wharf and Colin was carrying on a spirited conversation in sign language with a cheerful fat little man who promptly took us to his Chief, who spoke English.

Portugal is a Police State. The police officer took our passports from us and gave us little cards permitting us to go into the town. We were not to take anything ashore and we could collect our passports the day we left. It was all rather fierce and formal, but efficient and polite.

Before we went back to the Yacht Club, which we had spotted on the way in, we went for a little sail further up the Tagus to pay our respects to the full-rigged training ship of the Portuguese Navy. Also we went to have another look at the fregatos, the sailing barges of the Tagus, with their hooked bows like moorish slippers and single masts raked well aft. They are all most beautifully painted and decorated, and my, how well they sail.

At the Yacht Club we were greeted by the Secretary who showed us to our berth in Belem Basin among many large and famous yachts from all over the world. The police had telephoned him that we were coming and already there was an armed guard standing on the quayside with rifle and bayonet and a long bandolier of ammunition round his waist, to see that we did not bring anything ashore.

The Secretary asked if there was anything that we wanted.

'Yes, please', we said. 'We want to unload all our stores and gear ashore, then lift the boat herself on to the quay and paint her.'

He smiled quietly: 'The regulations, you know. But it can be arranged.'

He spoke to the guard, who nodded; then he came back to us.

'There is a store in the Club which you may use, and a crane in the corner. Please avail yourselves of our facilities while you are here.' Then he disappeared.

All next day we sweated in the hot sun, carrying great sacks of nylon sails, canned food, and all sorts of dutiable articles ashore, sometimes leaving them in great piles on the quayside.

It is a funny thing, but somehow the guard never noticed us. When we came by with our sacks over our shoulders he would turn to look at something behind him, gaze at the sky, or just stare at his boots, but he never did see us doing anything we shouldn't. And in the evening, when we went ashore, he would be there, guarding our boat for us. We began to appreciate the virtues of a Police State.

I must say, however, that the sentry was very efficient and had a good look at anything we were carrying so long as it was obviously perfectly innocent.

With much gesticulation and shouting a gang of workmen from the Club helped us to lift *Sopranino* out of the water and deposit her in a cradle among the little day sailing boats on the quay. Then we set about cleaning and painting her. Colin took charge of this while I made forays into the town to get food, stores, paint, charts, and other things that we might need in the unknown places ahead.

The simplest thing like buying a loaf of bread can present quite a problem in a strange land where you don't understand the language, and the simplest purchase is always the subject of spirited bargaining. But that is the life of the ocean voyager: a continuous succession of odd and unexpected problems.

Another curious and unexpected problem was the disposal of the things bought by accident.

Another characteristic of ocean travel is contrast. One night you are in a storm at sea, where your very life depends from minute to minute on your own skill and judgment, and the next you are lying in bed in a luxurious club. You may have your lunch, as we did, sitting on the ground in the shade of the boat in our old overalls, surrounded by pots of paint and scraps of used sandpaper, sharing a hunk of bread and a bowl of stew with a Portuguese workman.

Sopranino

And the same evening you will be all dressed up in your best, to be called for by a large limousine and taken to a glittering party, where you will dine with Crown Prince Umberto of Italy or one of the other Royal Personages in exile there.

Soon *Sopranino* was in the water again, all freshly painted, her gear and stores aboard, ready to go. Just then the owner of a fine large 12-metre racing yacht called *Sunday* approached Colin to ask him to design a deckhouse to convert her into a cruising boat. This meant money, so we stayed another week while Colin prepared the plans and then got ready to leave.

Sunday is the old American 12-metre Seven Seas. The drawings for the deckhouse were drawn between the cabins of three yachts in the harbour. When one went out for the day, I moved to the next, complete with set-squares and lengths of drawing paper and scales and compasses and dribbling drawing pins.

We made very many friends in Lisbon, both among the Portuguese and also among the large colony of English living there, and on the day of our departure they all turned out to see us off. There was a line of cars at the dock, including several diplomatic ones, and quite a crowd on the pier head, waving and taking photographs as we sailed out into the Tagus.

We sailed from Lisbon at the appointed hour in the afternoon. A planned departure, with a last bowl of porridge each and a very careful dressing up in oilskins, with elastic bands adjusted at the wrists and ankles to keep us dry for as long as possible, for there was a fine breeze and we should have to beat to windward out of the Tagus.

This care was of course the death of the breeze. Even as we took our first leg into the river it began to drop. But the tide was just starting to run out and with luck we would be swept out of the river with or without wind.

Sure enough we got swept out. The overfalls on the bar gave us a tossing. In the midst of them a large sailing schooner under motor caught sight of us and came over to see if we needed rescuing. To make quite sure, she came very close indeed. A large and probably unhandy schooner is not the ideal close companion for a little boat becalmed in the confused seas on a bar and we were pleased when eventually she waved happily and motored away.

Southward Ho!

As it grew dark the tide slackened and then began to turn. No wind arrived despite knives stuck in the mast, whistling, threats of fried supper and other seamanlike manoeuvres. We found ourselves slowly but surely retiring into the Tagus again.

The tide this time swept over sandbanks and we had to juggle with the ghost of a breeze produced by our own movement on the tide to edge ourselves clear. We tumbled over the bar again with a somewhat anxious eye on the bearings of the lights marking the channel. The tide swept us on up the Tagus and not a whisper of wind arrived.

We had seen the bar of the river Tagus by day and by night now and thought little of sweeping out again on the next ebb and, for all we knew, in again on the following flood. We could not anchor in the deep-water channel and so must make our way inshore.

The moment had come to give our hand-propulsion unit its first sea trials. We had on board, buried deep but not too deep, a fine oar blade which clamped on to the end of one of the spinnaker booms, thus making it into a sweep. Originally this was supposed to go in a rowlock in a socket on the stern. At Lisbon, however, Patrick had conceived of a scheme, and the socket was full of the lower end of a parrot perch complete with electrical parrot. So we bound up the sweep with cloth and tied it to the rail in such a way that we could take it in turns to row with both hands, while sitting on the tiller to steer.

My fine parrot was a home-made wind generator, consisting of an old bicycle generator with a propeller on it, fixed on the end of a pole. The idea was that it should go around in the wind and make electricity, but in practice it made more noise than anything else. Humming and squeaking away up there while the light got brighter and dimmer as we went up and down on the waves, until finally we decided that wind generators in little boats are not a practical thing at sea, and put it reverently to rest in a deep locker.

With much labour we made our way inshore and close to some anchored fishing boats. We dropped our small hook, played out all the fine string which we call our anchor cable, and turned our minds to serious things like supper and bunks.

Next morning we were lying asleep, anchored in the river waiting for the tide to go our way again, when we were

Sopranino

awakened by shouting noises. It was the British Consul, out in his yacht, come to see what we were up to. We told him our problem and he gave us a tow, down past the Gingerbread Castle, to the entrance of the North Channel.

Still there was no wind, so all that evening we sweated away, taking turns to row her, a hundred yards at a time, across Cascais Bay past Estoril, to anchor off Cabo Roca, where we lay waiting for a wind to take us to Africa.

CHAPTER FIVE

Fair Wind to Africa

*Fairy Stories—The Last Headland of Europe—A Storm Brewing—Casablanca,
Arabs, Riots, Camels—The Storm Arrives, Sinking the Kangaroo—Cherry Brandy—
Patrick Is Washed off the Sea Wall—Our Broadcast in French—We Run out of
Money—Away down the Barbary Coast—The Agadir Line—Colin Is Ill at Sea—
We Arrive in Las Palmas—Colin Goes to the Hospital*

A NCHORED there, waiting for wind, we turned on the radio.
Good; a fairy story. We have a thing about fairy stories.
It all started way back in the Bay of Biscay. One day, in the
Great Calm we happened to tune in to a serial in Children's
Hour, all about Wicked Knights and Good Knights and Castles
and Beautiful Princesses. We were so intrigued to know what
would happen next that for several days we had solemnly
stopped the ship at that time each day while we both scrambled
below to hear the next instalment.

*The state of being hove-to is strictly insidious and must be fought
strenuously. It is so easy just to push the tiller away from you and let
Sopranino do the rest. Then all the tiresome showers of spray stop,
the motion is easier, and you can get up and move around.*

Now we both lay back in our bunks, each with his bowl of
stew and his glass of muscatel, carefully following the plot of
this tale as it came drifting over the ether from faraway England, slowly swinging our glasses and our bowls from side to
side as our little ship rolled gently on the long Atlantic swells.

Next morning a little breeze came up from seaward. We
hauled up our anchor and sailed off down the Portuguese coast,
southward bound once more.

By midnight on Tuesday, October 30, we were rounding
Cape St Vincent, the last headland of Europe, and trimming
our sheets for Africa. It was here that in olden times fierce sea
battles between wooden ships had been fought with powder
and shot. Now, in the clear night, great steel ships ploughed

endlessly past us, following their peaceful business of taking passengers and cargo from the north to the south and from the east to the west.

At one moment, off Cape St Vincent, I counted no less than thirty-two ships in sight. For the most part they were Spanish trawlers, with their bright splashes of yellow paint, but there was a good round dozen of large and prosperous liners and cargo ships.

But we were not with them. We were with the ghosts of the sailing ships of old, sailing southward in search of the trade winds that would bear us across the ocean to the New World.

In the summer the trade winds extend right up the Portuguese coast, but in winter they move away down to the Canary Islands, off the African coast, and that was where we must go. But now we had to be careful, for the powerful southwesterly gales had moved into this area.

They last about four days, and then for about a week the weather will be fine, until the next gale comes along. Four days had gone by since the last one had finished, so we must hurry before the next one caught us. Now it was fine and sunny, with a nice steady breeze from the north to drive us on our way, but already there were signs in the sky of trouble to come. High feathery clouds climbed slowly across the sky from the southwest, innocent-looking heralds of an impending storm.

The night after Cape St Vincent was a magical night. A slight mist on the phosphorescent sea made a steel-blue sea fade into a steel-grey background, with the breaking tops of the seas flashing luminous green through the mist. Hannibal put it down to the muscatel.

By midday Thursday I reckoned we had fifty miles to go to Casablanca, on the African coast. Already the barometer was falling fast. The storm was coming closer every hour. In the afternoon the wind began to drop away; the calm before the storm was setting in. Whatever happened, we must not be caught on the infamous Barbary Coast when it came.

Just after dark, Casablanca light came up ahead of us, about eighteen miles away. Then Cape Fedala light, away to the eastward. We were closing in.

At three in the morning the wind died away altogether,

Fair Wind to Africa

leaving us becalmed about five miles from the harbour. Too far to row in the heavy swell of the coming gale; all we could do was to sit there, alert, on watch, and ready to take advantage of any little breath of wind to work our way into that harbour.

All through the morning we drifted slowly inshore, first in the cold and damp of the morning mist and later in the blazing heat of the African sun. Little by little we crept past the whistle buoy, squeaking away like a dying pig as it rose and fell on the rollers. And in the early afternoon we slid through the entrance, into the protection of the great sea wall. Now it could blow a gale if it wanted to, for all we cared.

Africa at last. More than a thousand miles from England. Land of camels, Arabs, and veiled women. Busily we set about preparing for our arrival. Hannibal came up on deck to pronounce his verdict on this new continent: 'No Elephants. Pfui!'

We told him there would be camels, but he was not interested in camels: 'How about a drink?'

'Excellent idea. We'll all have one', we agreed.

But as we drifted across the harbour, towards the little walled basin at the northern end, there was something strange about this place, something forbidding. It was too quiet; the air was full of a sort of pent-up tension. I had an awful feeling that something dreadful was going to happen at any moment. Not just the gale, but something animal—or human.

Inside the little basin three French destroyers were lying, their guns uncovered, while armed guards patrolled the quays and watched the gates leading into the docks. The port doctor's launch came over to us and showed us where to moor. He explained that they were having a little trouble in the town and it would be better for us to moor where we would be in the protection of the Navy.

Apparently it was election time, and the Communists were taking the opportunity to stir up trouble among the occupants of the native quarter. There had been a certain amount of shooting, he said, but rather more stoning and knifing. The French authorities were taking a very firm line, however. At

Sopranino

every street corner there was a truck full of soldiers, ready for
action, while all public buildings were guarded by sentries
with rifles and bayonets.

The docks were guarded and the Navy was standing by. We
were not to worry, but of course we must be careful when we
went into the town, and not go unarmed. And above all we
must stay away from the native quarter.

That night we met M. Tourniquet de Brandt, Commodore
of the little Yacht Club, and heard tales of people being knifed
to death for trying to interfere with robbers. We went to bed,
out on our mooring, with evil-looking types paddling silently
by in rowing boats.

Next morning the gale had arrived. Great seas were pound-
ing and booming outside the high sea wall, sometimes throwing
plumes of spray high above it. Even where we were, down in
the shelter of the surrounding buildings, the wind was blowing
and screeching and tugging at *Sopranino's* rigging. It jerked the
whole ship, trying to break her away from her moorings.

As the day wore on it swung around off the land, bringing
great clouds of dust and sand driving into the town. A man
went past in a small boat which was rapidly filling with sand.

Of course it was all my fault, for I had thoroughly hosed Sopranino
down, cleaned and polished her the day before.

'Sirocco!' he shouted. We made a note of that.

In the evening an amateur radio enthusiast came in his car
to take us to his shack, to try and get through to England. The
shack was a truly wonderful place: a small room, in an otherwise civilised apartment, full of weird and wonderful equipment. Tall steel racks, way up to the ceiling, held layer after
layer of naked radio sets, each overflowing downward on to
the next like nightmarish waterfalls. And evil-looking black
boxes lurked, humming and crackling to themselves, in dark
corners.

We sat in a row at a long wooden bench, littered with micro-
phones, Morse keys, loudspeakers, and little bits of radio
casually connected together by odd pieces of wire, while our
host pulled and pushed his knobs and switches like an organist

at a console. Some of the knobs that were out of reach he poked with sticks.

Out from the wall projected a long rod with a large wheel on the end of it. Each time he turned this wheel all the lights would dim and I had visions of the charred remains of his grandmother, baking away in a secret oven.

And all the time he was carrying on a disjointed conversation with his apparatus:

'Is that you, Brazil?... Hullo, Cape Town... Texas, be a dear and get off the line, I am trying to get England ... No. Not you, Germany, ENGLAND. ...'

'Un moment', he said, vanishing out of our circle of light, suddenly to reappear with an enormous bottle of cherry brandy. He poured out three large glasses: *'Santé!'*

'Santé', we said.

He poured out three more. ...

I don't think we ever did get through to England. I remember a long line of overlapping cherry brandy bottles, all empty, that would keep shuffling themselves together and fanning out again like a magician's cards, and then we were in *Sopranino*, lying in our bunks, while rain beat down on her decks.

It was light. I looked across at Colin. He looked awful. He opened his eyes, looked across at me, and quickly shut them again. Outside the rain was coming down in torrents, turning all the dust into mud. After awhile Colin got up and made some porridge. That was better. Then we struggled into our oilskins and went ashore.

It was not the odd glass of cherry brandy that produced our undoing so much as the sponge fingers. After perhaps the second glass our radio man disappeared, to return with a box of them. These, he explained, were at their best only when dunked in cherry brandy. And he was right. And it was a large box.

Next day we found a portable water-still on board with us and the only way we can explain it is that he must have given us that as well.

The local newspapers were full of the story of *Kangaroo*, the 240-ton schooner yacht owned by Freddie MacEvoy, that had just been wrecked about thirty miles up the coast. Apparently

73

they had come down from the Mediterranean and were going the same way as we were. But they had passed Casablanca and tried to carry on to the next port down the coast. That was their first mistake.

Then they had tried to get into port after the gale had started. That was their second mistake. You cannot afford to make two mistakes with a gale around, and now their fine ship was lying a mass of wreckage on the rocks, with four lives lost, including those of the owner and his wife.

On the whole, Casablanca was a depressing place to be in in a small boat, so as soon as the gale began to abate we set about cleaning up the mess and getting our boat ready for the next hop, to the Canary Islands.

The rioting had finished, but going into the town to shop was still quite a proposition. You took your shopping bag, dropped in your list of things to get, then took your gun, checked it, cocked it, and dropped it in too. You were now the well-dressed shopper.

The town itself is a weird mixture of the old and the new. Of fine modern buildings and squalid shacks. Of busy business-men in modern garb, tall tribesmen who look as if they have come straight in from the desert, and women in long flowing robes with veils over their faces.

Going into town you have to pass along one side of the native quarter, past the docks, before you reach the modern European section. This is all right in the day time, but you must be more careful coming home at night. If in doubt, the great thing is to take a firm line.

One evening we were coming home in the dark, when a man came up on a bicycle and asked us for a light for his cigarette. I took my gun out from behind my shopping bag and covered him, while Colin gave him his light. He thanked us politely and rode happily off. It's just the way you do things in those parts.

Then we did a silly thing. We should have known better, but we asked all the locals if the water was fit to drink.

'Certainly', they said. 'We drink it all the time.'

Fair Wind to Africa

So we drank it, and were promptly taken sick, both of us, with severe stomach trouble. Of course the people who live there have grown up with the stuff and seem to have developed an immunity to it, but it is quite full of every kind of microbe, and let a stranger take one glass of it and he will be flat on his back for a week.

We really ought to have been put off by the very appearance of the stuff as it trickled sickly out of the tap. A warm viscous liquid obviously crammed full of succulent, well-cared-for germs.

While we were sick, another ocean voyager, Collin Fox, came in from Fedala, about twenty miles up the coast. His partner had left him there, and now he was alone—a bright and cheerful fellow who would often invite us over to share the comfort of his comparatively large and luxurious cabin.

Collin Fox and I were just a touch embarrassed to see each other in Casablanca. The last time we had met was when I put Sopranino *on the hard at Lymington for a scrub, not long before we left.*

Another yacht was lying further up the hard, obviously finishing a repaint. I wandered up to have a look and to borrow a larger scrubbing brush, and inquired casually where they were going after the refit. Collin Fox said happily: 'Oh, think we might potter up to Holland. Nice place, Holland. Where are you fellows off to next?'

I replied: 'Um . . . May go to Belgium.'

Then up came another gale, another stinker. Once more great waves were hurling themselves against the sea wall that ran out parallel with the shore for over a mile, protecting the shipping that lay in its shelter waiting to come into the docks.

One evening when the gale was at its height, Colin and I went for a walk along that wall. It was one of those huge affairs with giant cranes on it, straddling two railway lines and a roadway that stretched across its width, while on the seaward side there was a further protective wall, about ten feet high, to keep the bigger breakers from coming across the roadway.

Out towards the end, spray was flying high over this little wall, leaving large wet patches on the roadway. Colin decided to turn back at this point, while I went on, as I wanted to go out to the end. I had hardly gone a hundred yards more when

Sopranino

I noticed two of the most enormous seas coming in one after the other. I stood and watched them, fascinated, as they merged together, piling up into a vast mountain of water, rolling steadily towards where I stood, alone on the wall.

Quite obviously the wall was not going to stop this lot. There must have been thousands of tons of water poised high above the wall, drawing themselves up into a great curling breaker which gathered speed as it came towards me.

It was too late to run for the nearest shelter, far down that bleak, wind-swept expanse of concrete. I flung myself down, facing the wave, got a good grip with my hands and feet on the railway lines, and waited.

Then it struck. With a thundering roar the whole top crashed over the little protecting wall and came sweeping across to me, green and solid. I thought of the unprotected edge behind me, where the main wall dropped sheer away to the rocks at its base, and hung on for all I was worth.

Then I felt my feet and my hands give, and I was sliding backwards towards the edge. As I went over I hung for a moment by my fingers, while the water thundered past over my head and dropped, crashing, on the rocks below. Then my fingers gave, and I was falling down, down. . .

There was a bump. Then a pause as I flew through the air again. Then another bump, and a slither, and a thud. I opened my eyes. I had stopped moving. I looked around. I was wedged in a crevice between two rocks, half in the water. I tried my arms and legs. They seemed to be working.

'Let's get out of here', I thought, 'before the next one comes.' So I climbed out of my hole like a rather surprised lobster, and swam away clear of the rocks. I was fully dressed, so off came my shoes for a start, then I reconsidered the matter.

I was not feeling so hot, and any minute things might begin to freeze up, so there was no sense in hanging around there. Time I went home; the game was getting rough. The water had finished pouring down the wall and the odds were that there wouldn't be another one like that for a few minutes. I decided to chance it, anyway.

Fair Wind to Africa

There was a nice flat rock over on my left, so I swam over to it and let the swell deposit me on it. Then I went straight up that wall. To this day I don't know how I did it, but one moment I was at the bottom and the next I was running along the road at the top, towards the cranes.

Further along I saw a little Arab motorboat coming out, with somebody in it, waving. It was Colin, coming to the rescue. I waved and he turned back, to meet me down by the docks. He looked white and shaken. He must have had a worse time than I did, watching me disappear over the edge, and wondering what the devil I was up to.

I was watching and saw the sea break over the wall and Patrick first drop on to the railway line and then get swept away and disappear over the edge. When the spray cleared I saw Patrick clear of the rocks and swimming.

I shouted and waved to him, and then rushed off up to the jetty where I remembered seeing a small launch. Down the steps to it, shouting 'au secours!' at the Arabs sitting there. I shouted at them in French and English, and probably Arabic and Hindu as well, undid all the lines, opened the engine case, and prodded the starter. They got the idea and set off around the corner, while I danced on the cabin top.

Around the corner there was no sign of anybody in the sea. All that was to be seen was a damp figure walking slowly back along the breakwater.

That evening I lay in my bunk, while Colin sat with the medical book open and a great pile of ointments and things, patching up the odd cuts and bruises.

Next morning I could not move. Nothing worked. Colin sat me up for my breakfast. That was fine, but if I lay down again I just had to stay there until he rescued me. I heard Collin Fox call over from his boat: 'How is he?' and through the hatch I saw Colin's hand, making the Thumbs Down sign. This really was a bore.

Furthermore, we had promised to do a broadcast over Radio Maroc that very morning. We could not let them down, so I was carted ashore and taken along to the studio.

The broadcast was fun. It was all in French, and the

77

Sopranino

announcer was a young and excitable French girl. All went well until we tried to explain precisely what Hannibal was all about. We got into a beautiful muddle trying to define the precise functions of a pink elephant, until, mercifully, they switched us off.

I think the best part of the story was the finish. The broadcast was recorded and was to be replayed as part of the programme at one o'clock. So we went along to a café we knew and ordered coffee and buns. We explained with care and our best French that we were to be on the air in a few moments. Everybody was suitably impressed and the knobs were turned to the right programme. The introductory pieces came and then the turn before ours. Then, as we began to compose ourselves and look modest, there was a small fizzing from inside the set and it all faded gently away, leaving only a thin wisp of smoke to rise slowly from the speaker.

Obviously I was in no condition to go to sea, and we couldn't afford money for doctors. However, the port health officer very kindly gave me a check-up and recommended me to the masseur at the local Turkish baths, who, he said, would straighten out the kinks. So there we went. He turned out to be a fine fellow who took the whole thing in his stride and, after a couple of visits to him, I was in working order again.

As a matter of fact it seems that I was lucky to get off as lightly as I did. We were told by the locals that four other men had had the same experience during the last couple of years, but unfortunately none of them had lived through it.

We still had to wait another week or so before I would be ready and fit to go to sea again, so we filled in time preparing the boat for the next passage and, in the evenings, we would go over and see Collin Fox or the Commodore.

The Commodore told us all about the local smugglers. There is quite a brisk trade going on at night all along that dismal coast, in everything from arms to narcotics. The French authorities know that it is going on and do their best to stop it, but they can't be everywhere at once. And wherever they aren't, the smugglers are.

One evening Collin Fox came back from the town with a

Fair Wind to Africa

brand-new pair of shoes, loosely wrapped in brown paper. As he came down the jetty, one of them slipped out of the paper, bounced off the jetty, and disappeared with a gurgle into the murky water off the dock. He started prodding around after it with a stick, and the more he couldn't find it the angrier he got, until finally he gave up and, taking the other shoe, he threw it far out into the dock. Next morning the tide was out, and there was the first shoe sitting serenely on the mud bank, within easy reach.

We heard a small commotion nearby and stuck our heads out of our little boat, to find him hopping up and down on the dock, airing his considerable vocabulary to an admiring audience of Arab boatmen.

By the time I was well again we had run right out of money. I remember that one hot sultry day we found we didn't even have the price of one Coca-Cola between the two of us. Our food was running short and we had over five hundred miles to go to the Canary Islands, where there should be about £50 waiting.

Even my reserves failed, and that meant that we were more than somewhat broke, for it was my canny habit always to keep a few francs or pesetas undeclared and in reserve for the ultimate Coca-Cola or what have you.

This time Collin Fox came to our rescue. He lent us £2, telling us to leave it for him in Las Palmas, to collect as he followed us through. We took our £2 up into the town and came back with a small piece of meat, some bread, and a large sack of vegetables. Now we could sail on our way.

We waited for the current gale to blow over and as soon as it had finished we prepared to leave, spending our last evening with Commander Bernicot, the distinguished French sailor, one of the four men in the world who had sailed alone through the Magellan Straits. He told us about a large shark that he had met off the northern tip of South America, where we should be going. It was nearly as long as our boat, and he described how he had shot it repeatedly at short range with a rifle. Each time it came back.

Sopranino

Finally he had tied a piece of pork to a chain to attract it, and then put the muzzle of his rifle against its head and shot it, but still he had not succeeded in killing it. He said that a shark has a very small brain, while all the rest is muscle. Unless you are lucky and hit the brain itself, you might as well save your ammunition. It all sounded very cheering.

I still have perfect confidence in my own (untried, thank God) method with sharks, which is to dose them with a hot rocket from my Very pistol. A green one, since green is unlucky at sea, or perhaps a red one with stars.

Then he went on to describe the weather conditions at that time of the year between Casablanca and the Canary Islands, our next passage. There is a line, called the Agadir line, that runs east and west through the town of Agadir, around latitude 30° north. Once across that line we should find good weather and favourable breezes, but between there and where we were the winter southwesterly gales would be building up.

If we could get down south between the gales and across the Agadir line, we should be all right. If not, well, anything could happen. They were still picking up the wreckage of *Kangaroo* down that way. We thanked him and turned in for a last night's sleep before setting out.

The following morning, Wednesday, November 21, Commander Bernicot came over to say that the weather was settling and he advised us to leave right away. As a parting gift he gave us his own copy of the pilot book for the Canary and Cape Verde Islands, which we had been unable to get. Just then there was nothing that could have been more valuable to us.

As we sailed out of the harbour around midday we passed literally dozens of ships, anchored outside, waiting their turn to come into the docks. The outer harbour was full of them and there were even more lying to their anchors outside. Trade was booming despite the unrest, and Casablanca must have been one of the busiest ports in the world at that time.

Outside the breeze was very light indeed. One of the dangers of the Barbary Coast to a sailing boat without power is that often in the evenings the wind will die, leaving you with no motive power, while the long Atlantic swells roll up on to

Fair Wind to Africa

the sandy shore. If you are not very careful those rollers can carry you to your destruction on the rocks, while you are unable to do anything about it.

It was important, then, to get well offshore. And I mean *well* off. For two whole days we sailed straight out to sea, until we were over sixty miles from the shore, before we squared away for the Canary Islands. Then, with a nice light wind from the north behind us, we were able to set for the first time the twin spinnakers, special downwind sails that we should be using for trade-wind passage, and see how they would work on our small boat.

Without the mainsail to steady us, the rolling was considerable, but we would just have to get used to that. She ran very well, but however we tried we could not make her steer herself. She would hold her course for a little while and then swing around and stop.

This was something of a disappointment, as steering when running straight before the wind is always the most tiring and unless we could make her steer herself we should be faced with maybe thirty or forty days of it on the Atlantic run. Over a period this might wear down the crew, leading to all sorts of dangerous complications.

I was very keen to get this thing ironed out before we started on the long haul, so after lunch on Saturday, when Colin went below for his sleep, I got him to leave me a large bag full of pieces of string and elastic, plus a few spare pulleys. Within a couple of hours *Sopranino* was steering herself very nicely, putting herself back on course each time an extra large wave swung her off it, while I stood in the hatch admiring the view.

I had followed our original scheme of leading the lines from the two sails through blocks and to the tiller. Then I had added a damping device and bias control, plus checks to limit the movement of the tiller, to keep her from over-correcting and swinging the other way. The whole contrivance looked like a cat's cradle, with little bits of string running in all directions, mostly with knots in them. But it worked. Another problem had been solved.

Sopranino

Now, instead of steering all the time, the watch on duty could sit and do odd jobs about the boat, just keeping a general look-out and every few hours going out to replace my bits of string as they wore through and broke.

Later Colin looked the thing over. As the practical man in the outfit he saw what was making the strings break and corrected it. First he moved the inner ends of the two spinnaker poles up the mast, to ease the strain on the downhauls, then he replaced my bits of string with strong lines, properly fitted, and we had the complete automatic steering gear that was later to take us for thousands of miles across the ocean without our touching the tiller.

By Monday we were sitting contentedly in a flat calm, about 270 miles from Casablanca, with another 270 to go to the Canaries. It is remarkable how one settles in to life aboard. In quiet periods of moderately fine weather, one is quite contented with one's daily round and in no particularly urgent hurry to be anywhere else. Which, in some circumstances, is a good thing: our total day's run for that twenty-four hours was exactly seven miles.

Then trouble struck, from the most unexpected quarter as it always does. On Tuesday morning Colin fell sick. He had washed his underclothes in a detergent solution, rinsing them several times and drying them before putting them on again. Now he had developed some sort of allergy to the stuff. Great blisters were coming up all over his body, causing severe irritation and getting worse all the time.

We were then over two hundred miles from the Canaries and the nearest doctor. The wind was light, drifting us along at two or three knots. Things did not look so good.

Next morning, Wednesday, he was worse. The blisters were spreading and getting larger, while the irritation was so bad that he could hardly get any sleep. This was a thing for which we had no immediate cure, so it was vital that we get him to a doctor as quickly as we possibly could.

Meanwhile we drifted slowly southward towards the Agadir line. If once we could cross that line, and pick up the easterly breezes, we might make it in time, but if a southwesterly gale should catch us before we crossed the line, anything could happen. We might be blown away back to Gibraltar or the Spanish coast, and if that should take place there was no telling what would happen to Colin.

And all the time, unknown to us, we had the cure on board. We found out later that the anti-seasick drug Avomine, similar to Dramamine, is also an anti-allergic.

That night the wind fell away still further, leaving us drifting along at one or two knots, while, sitting on watch at dawn I could see the high wind clouds creeping across the sky from the southwest. There was a gale working up and it could strike at any moment.

Colin's condition had deteriorated in the night and, to make things worse, we had not had a fix for several days, so that we were not certain of our position. If we were to miss those small islands out in the ocean and have to spend days looking around for them, he might not last out.

As the sun came up I took my routine slow look all around the horizon. And there, right behind me, sharp and clear in the morning light, were mountain tops. Wonderful! There was only one place they could reasonably be: the most northern of the chain of Canary Islands. We were dead on our course, with about 110 miles to go.

And what is more, we were well across the Agadir line. With any luck we should have Colin in the hospital in twenty-four hours. I gave him the cheering news and on we went. The wind came around to the southeast, rather against us, but with the spinnakers down and our mainsail and big jib set we were making a good four knots straight towards Las Palmas, where there would be doctors, and money to pay them with.

All that afternoon and evening we churned on to the southward, bouncing and throwing up spray as *Sopranino* shouldered her way through the confused seas; a school of porpoises kept us company, weaving to and fro under our bows.

Soon after dawn on Friday I could make out something ahead. I reached for the binoculars. Yes, more mountain tops.

Sopranino

Excellent things that should be fitted to all small islands. Gran Canaria this time, the island on which the port of Las Palmas lies. On we went through the morning, with the island slowly rising out of the sea ahead of us.

Quite a reasonable sort of island was in sight that morning, looking perhaps only twelve or fifteen miles away. As we sailed towards it, however, it did nothing on its part to get closer. It just grew and grew out of the sea all day.

Colin was full of Anadin now, which was taking much of the pain away and making him feel much better, but we could not keep him like that for long and I was worried lest he should suffer more lasting damage.

By lunch time we were within about six miles of the harbour, going fast in a good breeze, with the coastline clearly visible ahead of us. Then suddenly the wind died away completely, leaving us drifting around in circles, rolling in the swell.

All that afternoon and all that night we lay there, within sight of the harbour, and it was not until eleven the next morning that we finally rounded the breakwater and drifted across to the docks.

As soon as we had cleared health and customs I took Colin up to the British Seamen's Hospital. The matron on duty took one look at him and telephoned for a doctor to come right away. A quick examination and he decided to operate. Soon Colin disappeared into the operating room, while I returned to the boat to await the outcome.

A fine hospital for seamen with Spanish doctors and English nurses. I was quite pleased to see it.

When they wheeled me into the chamber I was somewhat intrigued to spot an immense bone-handled corkscrew prominently displayed in the cabinet of sterilised instruments. While I was thinking that one out, the doctor cut himself with his own knife, which cheered me a little.

He got his own back by having a dummy run on the anaesthetic, letting me count into the hundreds before discovering that they had pumped water into me instead of whatever they were supposed to use. Next time, however, I only got to five.

When, next day, I became conscious of things again, I first noticed

Fair Wind to Africa

that the patient opposite was being firmly reproved by the Matron for staying out late at nights. An enormous Norwegian in the next bed was smoking a monster cigar. Another patient had apparently been playing that game so dear to merchant seamen, where one has a sledge hammer with which he steadily hammers the deck, whilst the others play at being the last hand from under before it strikes. My fellow-patient had scooped the kitty.

Back at the hospital in the morning I found him sitting up in bed looking much better. They had sorted out the immediate trouble and now they were doping him up with something to clear the matter up once and for all.

In the next few days he got steadily better and each time I visited him he told me tall tales of the other patients in the hospital until, after about a week, they let him out. Meanwhile I had caught Canary Fever, which is one more version of the old water-drinking trouble, so we decided to take a week's rest to recuperate before getting down to the job of preparing to cross the Atlantic Ocean.

CHAPTER SIX

Over the Western Ocean

*Preparing for the Atlantic Crossing—No One Has Ever Tried It—Patrick Finds a
Store—Our Anchor Is Stolen—Apology from the Thieves' Union—A Dog, a Cock,
and a Pig—Last Sight of Land for a Month—We Find the Trade Winds—
Both Sick: Poisoning?—A Theory about Waves—Learning to Navigate—Point
of No Return—Settling in—A Quarter of the Way Across*

THIS was it. Our jumping-off place. When we sailed from
Las Palmas it would be direct for Barbados, nearly three
thousand miles away across the ocean, with no land of any kind
in between. Five times as long a passage as we had ever
attempted in our little boat, and many times longer than anybody living had ever attempted in so small and light a craft.

I kept thinking of the time, way back in England, when I had
gone around to all the acknowledged experts on boats and the
sea, to ask their advice on various points. Time and time again
I had received the same answer to my questions: 'We don't
know. Nobody knows. No one has ever tried it.'

This, then, was real adventure. Going out into the unknown,
with one's life in one's hands, to find out the answers.

But first we must prepare. Once we were away and gripped
in the powerful grasp of the trade winds, there could be no
changing our minds, no turning back. If anything was wrong,
we should have to put up with it, maybe for weeks or months
on end, out there in the lonely wastes of the sea. And if it was
too wrong . . . well, anything could happen.

So we must prepare, and prepare well. Every detail must be
checked, every possible emergency that might conceivably
arise must be thought of now and the equipment prepared to
meet it.

First we must take everything out of the boat and into a
store. What store? We were alone in a strange and foreign
land, with no money to spare to rent stores.

Over the Western Ocean

'Well, you're the Organiser. Organise something', Colin remarked cheerfully. So off I went, through the cobbled streets lined with palm trees which cast round black shadows in the fierce midday sun. I went to the British Consulate, to see the Consul.

She turned out to be a charming and attractive girl. Things were looking up. And what is more, she gave me an idea. Two ideas, to be accurate, but the one that we are concerned with now was to go and see a Mr Kenny Staib, who had a large and delectable basement.

Feeling rather lost and lonely in his large and beautifully panelled office, I hesitated, then said:

'My friend and I were thinking of sailing over to Barbados in our nineteen-footer and we'd like to bring our gear ashore to look it over. Er . . . you wouldn't by any chance have a basement. . . ?'

Kenny turned out to be Norwegian and a sailor at heart, with his own yacht. Furthermore, he had an English mother and had married an English girl.

'Certainly', he said. 'Come and have a look at it.'

Downstairs he led me into a fine large storeroom, quite empty except for a couple of boats and a man in the corner hammering nails into a crate. It couldn't have been better.

'Here's the key. Use it whenever you like.' The man was a gentleman. I ran half-way back to the boat, then slowed down and strolled casually over to Colin, sat down on the wall and idly watched him working in the blazing heat, swinging my legs to and fro.

He looked up: 'Well?'

Triumphantly I dangled the keys in front of him. We had our store.

For two days we went back and forth, back and forth, taking every single thing out of that boat into the store, right down to the floorboards and every removable piece of rigging. For once she was stripped we would have to sleep ashore, and then the thieves would move in and go over her like a swarm of locusts. Anything that we didn't remove, they would.

Sopranino

The thieves are particularly enterprising in Las Palmas. They even steal the funnels off ships. A lawyer whom we met told us that a man came into his office one day to try and sell him the funnel of a ship that was lying in the harbour. He explained that it would be a little more expensive than usual, as the bolts were stiff. But that is Las Palmas.

Not only the funnels. They steal whole ships. Not long before we got there, they had been found raising steam in their second ship of the evening.

The next problem was where to sleep. There were two other ocean voyagers in the harbour, a couple of American boys named Jim and Joe, who were going our way in their thirty-six-footer, *Festina*. They had found themselves a room in a cheap hotel and took us along there.

It was quite a place. Our room for two, with wash basin, cost half-a-crown a night, and compared with *Sopranino's* cabin it was sheer luxury. Not that I wish to belittle *Sopranino's* cabin, mark you; on a wild night at sea there's no place I'd rather be, but after long months of living in that confined space it was a joy to be ashore for a while. True, the last occupant had left a pile of empty drug capsules in the drawer, and there *was* a goat on the roof opposite, but who cares about a little thing like that when the wind is in the east?

They also showed us their favourite restaurant, where for half-a-crown two of us could have a good meal, with wine. Etiquette demanded that one leave one's lorry outside, but after a while they came to accept us ocean voyagers as a kind of seagoing lorry-drivers. How right they were.

Day after day and week after week we painted, cleaned, checked, and counted. Every tiny detail had to be gone over thoroughly. We even stripped the labels off all our cans of food, painted them white to prevent them from rusting through if they got wet, and then painted code letters on them so that we would know what was in them. There comes a time when you get sick of stew made with marmalade instead of meat.

And only one mistake in the whole lot. A tin of sausages labelled 'grapes' and a complementary pair. Perhaps it counts as two mistakes.

Over the Western Ocean

Anyway, one morning we had a double dose of grapes and on another we could not face two lots of sausages.

Even with all this fine system, there remained at first an exciting element of doubt as to what the other fellow did have in mind when he labelled a tin 'M.S.' Now is it Meat Soup, or Marmalade Seville, or Mixed Stew, or Milk Sweet?

Water was a serious problem. The local stuff was not safe unless we boiled every drop of it. And then, what would happen if the stove should fail? True, we had two stoves in case one should fail, but still, water is the most vital thing of all on such a trip, and we couldn't be too careful about it.

And Patrick is a serious problem with water. He will drink the stuff neat anywhere in the world—with frightful results, Hannibal and I are agreed.

Eventually we found a brand of sparkling mineral water called Firgas that was said to be safe, so I bought cases and cases of the stuff and filled all our hundred aluminium water pots with it. Now our only worry on that score was whether it would combine with the aluminium to form poisonous salts, or corrode its way through and get out.

The Firgas sellers were distinctly uneasy about letting anyone have so much water at once. Probably they thought we were off on a bender.

One Sunday Kenny and his wife came down to take us away from it all to ride with them in their car to the top of a mountain. From there we could see far too much sea. It just seemed to go on and on in every direction, dwarfing even this large island. Hurriedly we came down again, back to the harbour.

The big American yacht *Sunbeam* had just come in, and we took a dinghy out to investigate. When we were half-way there, a voice called out of the darkness: 'Hey, there, *Sopranino*, come aboard'.

It was Tony Needham, who had come with me on the first run to Spain and back. He was working his way out to Nassau as part of the crew.

Tony was a compass adjuster, so I gave him our barometer to fix. We should want it, to warn us of hurricanes out there beyond range of the weather forecasts. With the casual air of the expert he opened it up, probed around inside it with a fork and said: 'It'll probably work now'.

Next morning we ran into a couple of young chaps looking lost. They were from South Africa, and had sold off all their belongings and come thousands of miles to join a boat that had not shown up on a world cruise. We introduced them to the skipper of *Sunbeam* and they were off to the Virgin Islands.

Then came a letter from Mike in England, to tell us that he and Pat Noakes, whom he had met with us the day before we left England, were getting married. Before this trip was over their first child was to be born.

Meanwhile Jim and Joe were having difficulties with the Spanish authorities. Off the African coast they had been invited aboard a Spanish military transport for a drink and now they had a salvage claim for some £120 against them that they couldn't possibly pay. An armed guard had been put on their boat and part of the engine removed.

They discussed the matter with an influential Spanish friend and he got to work. They were invited to a cocktail party to meet the Admiral's daughter. Next day the claim was reduced to £60. Then cocktails with the General's daughter, and it came down to £30. This went on until it was down to £2 which they paid and quickly sailed away, with two Spanish fishermen aboard as crew, for Caracas.

One way and another, that week, there was more going on on that remote island than you expect to find in Victoria Station in the rush hour.

Then it was our turn for a bit of excitement. About ten o'clock at night a messenger came rushing up to the hotel to tell us that *Sopranino* had gone away. We ran down to the quay. She was not there. Where she had been lying to her anchor, out in the harbour, there was now just an empty space on the water.

Frantically we ran around the wharfs and quays. Had anybody seen a little blue boat go out of the harbour? Nobody had. Then another message: a fisherman had found her, adrift in the harbour, bumping up against a stone wall. We dashed over to see her, fearing that she might be badly damaged. But she was all right. She had been saved in time, with just a few scratches on her paint to show for it all.

Sopranino *is the most sensible boat I know. Left to herself, she always does the right thing.*

We examined the anchor warp, hanging loose from her bow. It had been cut. Someone had cut her adrift to steal the anchor. Our turn had come to be robbed and, since there was nothing else to take, they had taken the anchor. In the time that we were in Las Palmas every single yacht was robbed at least once, so perhaps we were lucky.

The next morning, in a roundabout way, we received a message from the Thieves' Union. They were sorry, they said, that this had happened. No respectable thief would do such a thing. It must have been somebody from out of town. But we didn't get our anchor back. We shouldn't be needing it in the deep ocean anyhow, so eventually we sailed without one.

As the weeks of preparation went by we came to know the place quite well. Gran Canaria is a high, round, brown island, almost cone-shaped, with a little island called the Isletta, just off its northern tip. The harbour lies between the two, with its own little town around it. You can take the bus a few miles south along the coast to Las Palmas proper, but that is just one more large town.

Our little town was far more fun. The wild canaries are green, of course, but the tourists who come in on the ships want to buy yellow canaries to take back and show the folks at home, so naturally the locals oblige them by catching ordinary sparrows and dyeing them yellow. Then they appear on the quayside, just as the cruise ships are sailing away, selling them for four hundred cigarettes each.

I have not yet got over finding that Canaries are dogs. The Canary Islands are named after the dogs that were to be found there when the islands were discovered. Gran Canaria *translates itself to* 'The Island of Big Dogs'.

They breed camels there, too, and export them to Africa.

Sopranino

It is quite common to see a spare camel tethered to the railings, while its owner is in a café having a drink.

The local fishermen, who live aboard their large sailing fishing boats, cluster together in bunches out in the middle of the harbour for mutual protection against the thieves. Each boat carries a dog, a cock, and a pig. The dog is to warn them of approaching thieves, the cock to wake them up in the morning to go fishing, while the pig is kept in case they get lost at sea. Then they throw it overboard and it will always swim towards the nearest land.

The dogs, to my mind, are a little too highly bred. They must scent the thieves approaching in ocean liners five miles out to sea, and generally keep hard at their task, especially in the small hours.

We were never consciously nervous about the idea of setting out across the ocean, though we worried a great deal over the details. But around the time when preparations were almost complete, we both began to get edgy and difficult, so probably there was some kind of subconscious strain building up.

On Christmas Eve about eleven at night I was typing away in a deserted shipping office as usual, while Colin was finishing off his day's work aboard the boat, when quite unexpectedly Kenny appeared, to take us both home to join his family in their Christmas party. Soon we were sitting around a fine table in their luxurious home, enjoying a wonderful party.

At one moment I was sitting on a wall in the dark, waiting for the tide to rise and float Sopranino, *whose bottom we had been painting. It was not really so dull, for every now and then I would be challenged by a sentry with a fine line in modern weapons. We had picked out the best wall in the neighbourhood for the job and laid* Sopranino *against it, and the tide had dropped before it became apparent that it was a Government wall.*

Explaining just why I was sitting on their wall in sign language in the dark had its moments. But as I was saying, at one moment I was sitting on a wall in the dark waiting for the tide to rise, and at the next in the middle of Christmas.

Later they took us home to our pension, with the drug capsules in the drawer and the goat on the roof. And that is the way of the ocean voyager in port. Nothing is unusual. Your friends drift in from Denmark and as casually sail away to Caracas. You live in the cheapest dockside boarding house, counting your pennies to see if you can afford a bar of chocolate between you. Then for a brief moment you are the centre of attraction at a luxurious party; and when it's over, back you go to your boarding house.

It was Thursday, January 10, when we checked our passports and papers, clearing the ship for Barbados, and stepped aboard, ready to go. A last-minute check revealed that the batteries were leaking. They had been over-filled and there was enough free acid in the bilges to rot the ship apart.

Back ashore to drain off half the acid, a quick lunch, and we were ready. Then up came a squall, so strong that our Red Ensign was shaking the whole ship like a dog with a rat, while the barometer dropped like a stone. There was no point in getting everything wet at the start. Once we were away we would have to take the weather as it came, but now we could afford to wait one more day and start in comfort.

Colin lay in his bunk reading *The Pursuit of Love*, while I fiddled with the radio. All night we took it in turns to keep watch for thieves, sitting in the hatch and pointedly flourishing a large and fearsome-looking Very pistol while the other slept. Then, when it was light, we both got some sleep.

In the middle of my watch I noticed that a small yacht moored close by had disappeared. The thieves got the credit for this until I set off in a dinghy and found her on her way ashore, all by herself, with a frayed mooring rope.

When we awoke it was bright and sunny, with a nice easterly breeze. This was it, then. It is supposed to be bad luck to sail on a Friday, but we had waited long enough. Up with the P Flag. 'All persons should repair aboard. The ship will sail within the hour.'

Kenny saw the flag from his office window and came out in a dinghy to see us off. At 5.30 in the afternoon we hoisted our sails, let go our mooring, and drifted quietly across the harbour, leaving Kenny alone in the middle, waving us goodbye.

Sopranino

I can remember feeling sorry for Kenny, leaving him all alone in the middle of the harbour whilst we sailed away. We had watched Jim and Joe leave, and knew how it felt.

Across the harbour an official launch came chuffing over. A man in uniform came out on deck: 'Where are you bound?'

'Barbados', we shouted.

He raised his hat in solemn salute and slowly chuffed away.

As the sun went down the lights of Las Palmas came on one by one behind us, reminding us of our little restaurant and our hotel and all the people we knew there, while ahead all was darkness. There was nothing out there, nothing but sea and more sea for almost three thousand miles.

Slowly the island got smaller and smaller in the brilliant moonlight, until the dawn came up. Even then it hung there for a while, like a low cloud on the horizon, until finally it dipped below the surface of the sea and was gone. We were away. Off to the southwest to find the trade winds.

At first we were in the shipping lanes, with great ships on either side of us, bound away south for Cape Town and the Indian Ocean. Then, one by one, they left us alone on the sea, and we began to settle down to the long weeks of sailing ahead.

It is a funny life. One day an island will rise out of the sea ahead of you, like the fairy castle in a child's story-book. Within two days you are a part of that place. You have your own pet restaurant and bars; people hail you as you walk down the street, and as time goes on you get to know all about the private life of the girl behind the counter in the sweetshop.

Then suddenly, one day, you sail away. And all that life and all those people sink into the sea behind you, as if they had never been. Then for a while you will be alone on the sea, seemingly motionless, until the next place comes up and you start all over again.

After all the preparation and the excitement of setting out, our first reaction was one of disappointment, almost. We were having a very nice sail, but it did not really feel any different, out there, from the way it usually felt. Bowling along in a nice fresh breeze, bouncing gaily over the sea with no land in sight

94

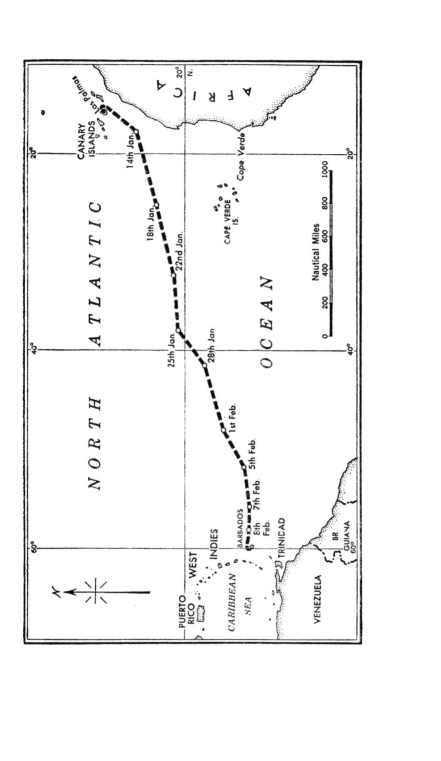

Sopranino

—this we had long ago come to accept as a normal way of life.

But of course neither of us had ever sailed in the trade winds, and we had not reached those yet. From questioning everyone we met who had been that way, we had a fair idea of what they were like, but of course nobody knew how a little boat like ours would behave in those conditions.

Some experts had told us that the motion would be so wild that it would wear out the crew long before we reached the other side; others that the breaking tops of the waves would continually be swamping us, until we wore ourselves out with bailing. Soon we should see for ourselves. It was all immensely interesting.

We had been told that when we did hit them there would be no mistaking them. They would arrive suddenly and forcefully. To be more exact, they were there all the time, but we should run into them. For thousands of years the northeast trades had blown across this part of the Atlantic Ocean, in a belt about a thousand miles wide, moving up and down a little with the seasons but always blowing strongly and steadily, day after day, week after week, year after year, from Africa towards the West Indies.

Suddenly we ran into them. On Sunday we were sailing quietly along in light variable winds, when we came to a long line of dark rainclouds, running straight across the sky from east to west. As we passed under them the wind hesitated for a moment, then came up out of the northeast, a fine strong blustery wind, dead behind us, throwing us forward urgently over the waves.

We were going fast, but the motion was wild. We would skid along on the face of a wave for a few seconds, the whole ship vibrating as the fin keel roared and trembled beneath us, until it broke around us in a smother of glistening foam and we dropped down, rolling in the hollow behind it. Then the next one would pick us up, and so we would go on.

As each wave came up behind us it would tower over us for a moment, high and blue and menacing, then up would go *Sopranino's* tail and off she would go, on the face of it. So far so

96

good. It was as we had hoped; she was so light that she was riding clean over the tops of them without taking anything aboard.

The fatigue angle was another matter, though. Steering was tiring and every little job became much more difficult to do, while hanging on with one hand as she rolled and swung over the seas. The solution was good food and lots of sleep, and that was where the self-steering gear would come in.

For another day we carried on like that, keeping on down to the southward to make sure that we were well and truly in the trades before we set the twin spinnakers.

Once they were set and the self-steering took over, things became much better. We called the steering gear Harry, after Harry Lime, the Third Man. Actually it was worth more than two men, for it worked steadily, day and night, week after week. And what is more it never fell sick and didn't eat anything.

We still kept regular watches, but now we could do odd jobs about the ship when we were on watch—cooking, navigating, and doing repairs—while the watch below got his full quota of undisturbed sleep.

We ourselves had always been sick the first day out, and then it passed over. But this time it had not passed over. Three days out we were neither of us at all well, both feeling sick and headachy. That might mean one of several things.

With the wind behind us, although it was strong enough to whistle in the rigging as we ran before it, we were not getting as much ventilation in the cabin as we were used to. It could be that.

It might be the unusually wild motion, or the reaction from the excitement of setting out on the Long Hop. Or again it might be some kind of poisoning, either from some food or from the water. It would have to be watched very carefully, anyway, for such are the things that bring disaster in small boats.

To add to our discomfort, every now and then a cross sea would come and swing *Sopranino* around with a lurch, chucking a dollop of spray down the hatch, all over everything.

Sopranino

For a long time I sat and thought about this sickness problem, and then I had an idea. We had painted our packets of porridge with white paint to prevent the damp from getting at them. It was possible that the oils from the paint had found their way through into the porridge and were affecting us. Anyway, I threw the packet we were using overboard and changed over to some other stocks that we had in aluminium bottles. It was worth a try.

Below, in the cabin, one's impression of sailing under these conditions was of being lurched and chucked around. She was behaving rather like a mad tram, and all the time, no matter what you were doing, you had to hang on or wedge yourself with your knees; otherwise you would soon find yourself flat on your face the other side of the cabin.

As each of us came on watch, he would put on his oilskins and sit in the hatch ready to go on deck if anything should happen. Every quarter of an hour he would stick his head out for a good look around, and in between times he would do odd chores such as washing up or peeling potatoes.

Peeling potatoes was normally a fine, interesting task. It had to be accomplished either completely with one hand or in the odd seconds gained by jamming the tiller against your leg whilst you took an odd swipe at the potato, and then back to the tiller before you were sufficiently off course to get spray over you.

Now that we were not having to steer we both found that we had a strong tendency to lethargy. We would just sit and stare at nothing. And do nothing. This would have to be dealt with firmly.

We each had six-and-a-half hours' straight sleep, an unheard-of luxury at sea, to celebrate the advent of the self-steering, and then we sat together in the cabin, regarding the grey, bleak, wet world outside with distaste. We had been off porridge and water for a couple of days and had been taking vitamin and ascorbic acid tablets. Colin was still rather ropy and I was having trouble with sores that were coming out on my neck, but neither of us seemed to be getting any worse, which was something.

Over the Western Ocean

Our fine Spanish doctor of the Canary Islands had given us his advice on the use of our big bag full of medical gear. He had produced a tube of ointment and a box of pills, saying:

'If anything goes wrong outside, put some of this ointment on it, and if anything appears upset inside, take some of these pills.'

And how very well it worked. We were better than new after a month of this treatment.

We found that the liquid in the cans of vegetables went quite a long way in supplying our needs, and when we checked on Wednesday, we found that we had only used a pint of water between us in twenty-four hours. We resolved to have a wash in fresh water when the log reached five hundred miles, if all went well.

We had then gone some three hundred miles, and were letting the wind take us out to the westward whenever it swung that way. We got a final bearing on Villa Cisnero radio beacon, on the African coast, before we ran out of its range, which indicated that we were only getting three or four miles of drift a day. Not as much as we had hoped for.

Little things were beginning to wear through already. Each day Colin would make a thorough inspection of all the gear and rigging, replacing things as they wore out. Mostly it was due to chafe as things rubbed against each other with the wild motion, but we were very glad that we had brought plenty of spares with us.

On Thursday the log reached four hundred. We were doing a hundred miles a day, which is good for a small boat. I came on watch and sat for a while considering our position. We were now well and truly in the trade winds, and the time had come for us to turn off to the westward. Colin was still not well—he had been sick twice in his last watch—and I was not feeling so good myself. On the other hand we were not getting any worse, the ship was going well, and the food and water were lasting out nicely. It had taken us months and months of hard work to get her down here. . . .

What the hell! We'd have a go. I went out on deck and swung her around to the west, towards America.

99

Sopranino

I went below and sat down, feeling much better now that I had made my decision. There was a clonk. And a clink. Then a clink-clonk. Something was loose in a locker, somewhere. It's the most infuriating sound. It wouldn't be so bad if it was regular and steady, but it never is. Each time you think that it has stopped it will do one more clonk. Or clink. Until you could scream.

Now it is odd, but clinks and clonks down below meant nothing to me. If they were bad I would attend to them, in case anything should break or chafe through the ship, but otherwise I had more important things to do, such as hitting the sack. On the other hand, little bumps or rattles on deck are incredibly infuriating and I must have spent hours tracking them down. A wire drawing across another at the top of the mast can produce the most teeth-setting scrape down in the sound-box of the hull.

You put your head between your knees, level with the food lockers, and listen, swaying from side to side like a drunken ostrich. Nothing happens. Not a sound. Then you sit up, red in the face but triumphant, and it starts again. Quite apart from the fact that it is rapidly driving you crazy, whatever-it-is will probably break soon and smother everything with jam or something equally revolting.

Finally you slide into your bunk, turn over, lie on your face and poke furiously about in the lockers until it stops. Then you creep quietly back into a sitting position, praying that it won't start again in *your* watch.

There was great excitement over lunch that day. With any luck we should make the five hundred miles tomorrow and have our wash in real fresh water. Salt water is all very well in its way, but it leaves you feeling sticky and you never quite seem to get dry again after it. Fresh water is, of course, by far the most precious commodity aboard a little boat at sea. A man can live for ten to fourteen days without food, but he will die within four if he runs out of water.

When we started out we had forty days' food and fifty days' water, for an estimated crossing time of thirty-five days. We had our daily ration of one quart of water a day each, for all purposes, and usually managed to save enough of that for a shave every second day, using the dry shaver in between times. But we also had a water schedule, based on miles made good towards our destination, and when we ran ahead of schedule we would declare a bonus and have a wash.

And on Friday it came up: five hundred miles. Each in his turn retired below with his precious bowl of water. First he would clean his teeth and have a shave in it. Then he would wash his way slowly and luxuriously from his head downwards, finally dabbling his feet in it. By which time it was about ready to be thrown overboard.

These little things may sound trivial to anyone sitting ashore, surrounded by taps full of fresh water, but out there on the ocean they are of vital importance in keeping up the morale of the crew and thereby ensuring the safety of the ship.

All our water was, of course, the fizzy Firgas stuff. I tried a glass of it neat; it smelt funny but tasted all right. Getting a cup to drink it out of was quite a game, though. I removed the flag that wedged the cups in their net, took one out, but was not quite quick enough in getting the flag back. The ship rolled, and all the other cups came rushing out, flying around the cabin like birds. It took me several minutes to catch them all and get them back in their net again.

In the excitement and turmoil of leaving Las Palmas I had been guilty of the most heinous crime a navigator can commit. I had forgotten to wind the chronometer, and it had stopped. Now, before we could find out where we were, we had to re-rate the thing from the time signals on the radio.

One day we would miss the signal, the next day it would be too faint to hear, then it would come through loud and clear and we couldn't find the stop watch, until it became quite a thing in our lives.

The weather forecasts were fun. They were coming from the BBC, full of tales of horror about southerly gales all around the coasts, while where we were it was hot and sunny, with a blue sky dotted with fleecy white clouds, too like a picture post-card for words.

We measured the waves. From where we sat they looked

Sopranino

quite large, rushing up behind us; one might easily have guessed them to be twelve to fifteen feet high. But in fact they were averaging nine feet, which shows how easily you can be misled. Even so, nine-footers are sizeable fellows and not to be trifled with, as any small-boat sailor will agree.

There is a formula for the maximum size that the waves will normally attain in deep water. Their height, in feet, should not exceed the square root of the distance that they have come from the shore, in miles. That is to say that 400 miles offshore you are likely to get 20-foot waves; 900 miles off, 30-foot waves; 1600 miles off, 40-foot waves; and 2500 miles off, 50-foot waves.

Since, then, the trade winds blow from Africa towards the West Indies, and there is no land in between, we could expect the waves steadily to increase in size as we went along. On the other hand, I reckoned that the ship would be getting lighter as we used up our supplies of food and water, so that she would still be able to ride them. It was an interesting point, anyway, and we should soon know the answer.

Thus it became a mark of virtue to eat large meals and so lighten the ship.

At last we got our time signal. The chronometer was behaving itself, so now we could find out just where we were. That is to say we could try. For, though we had both had quite a bit of experience in coastal and short-run navigation—using dead reckoning, radio, and the occasional simple noon sight on the sun for latitude—neither of us had ever done any serious astro-navigation.

We had a sextant and a chronometer, and lots of interesting books full of figures, but we had never really got down to learning how to use them. This approach is traditional in the best Ocean Voyaging circles, and anyway it seemed reasonable to assume that we should have plenty of time to learn before we hit Barbados.

So on Friday, a week after we had left Las Palmas, I decided to have a shot at it. Out came the sextant, and we took two sights on the sun, one at noon and one at three in the afternoon. Sixteen minutes later it was all worked out, and after that we had no more trouble. It really is amazingly simple. Of course we used the R.A.F. tables, which were worked out for quick and easy reference in aircraft during the war, and they are not quite as accurate as the full tables used in big ships, but they are well within the limits of the accuracy with which you can take a sight in a little boat at sea.

In practice we found that this method would give us our position within a couple of miles either way, which is quite good enough to take you to your landfall, particularly as a small boat is so much more manoeuvrable than a ship, being capable of turning or stopping almost in its own length in normal conditions.

We were now some six hundred miles from Las Palmas and we took out the charts to plot our position. They were a horrid sight, nothing but sea and more sea for hundreds of miles in every direction.

This was our Point of No Return. Up to this point we had the choice of turning to the southeast and running for the Cape Verde Islands, some six hundred miles away, but from now on that would no longer be a practicable proposition. You can go across the trade winds, but to attempt to go against them for any distance would be a waste of time.

The ship was going well, particularly since Colin had made some further adjustments to the twin spinnakers, so that she was keeping a better course and going faster. We ourselves were both beginning to feel better, so the chances were that our sickness of the last few days had in fact been due to the porridge.

We checked our supplies of food and water. Everything was going according to plan. We carried straight on out to the westward. From now on there could be no turning back. It would have to be the West Indies or . . . nothing.

Incidentally, the greatest difficulties of working out a sight, as of everything else that we did, were purely physical. To sit at a desk with pencil and paper, with all the different books open at the right pages around you, is one thing. But with the books sliding and jumping around, flipping over a page or two in the process, it is quite a different proposition. If you put your pencil down for a moment it would fly off the chart table, to disappear among the cans on the locker below, or even in the one on the other side. You had to arrange your open books cunningly, one overlapping the other, holding the last one down with your elbow. Then, when you were all set, a sheet of water would come down the hatch, splut!, all over everything, and you would have to set about mopping up the mess and drying everything out before you could continue.

But every day we learned a new trick, and little by little we began to settle down to life on the ocean. Not having to steer, we had time to do things: wash our socks, fish, or just lie in the sun on the foredeck.

One of our daily tasks was the washing of the dish towels. These were towed for one hundred miles and then declared clean by common consent. It worked admirably, if you discount the general yellow colour and the ragged edge of the towel we towed for two hundred miles by mistake.

We had discussed the possibilities of sunstroke with the doctors before we left England, and had been told that the best thing to do was to build up a tan, which would protect us from the sun's rays. So each day we would take our shirts off and sunbathe a little, starting at twenty minutes a day and slowly building up, to avoid peeling and losing it all.

By now we were around latitude 22 degrees north, well in the tropics. The sun was blazing down out of a clear blue sky nearly every day, with quite a bit of bite in it. When the decks were dry, the dark portions were uncomfortably hot to touch, though the light-coloured surfaces were all right, as they didn't absorb so much heat. Below in the cabin the temperature was running about 75 degrees around midday.

When we had been planning the trip we had gone into the question of colours very carefully, as we had everything else. *Sopranino* had to be smart, to create a good impression in foreign ports, and at the same time as efficient as we could possibly make her.

For the topsides, white would be no good, as it shows every

mark and would soon look dreadful after knocking around in a few commercial ports. Dark colours were out, as they would absorb the heat and cause her to open up and leak in time. So it had to be a pastel shade. Pink looks wrong on the water, green is unlucky, so it had to be blue.

The decks were painted cream, to reflect as much light as possible without being quite so glaring for the eyes as dead white, and the bottom was coated with several layers of worm-resistant preparations, followed by two coats of the standard red anti-fouling to prevent the growth of weed which would have slowed us down.

Only the upper works and hatch, which we would be continually coming into contact with, were kept varnished for ease of cleaning.

Our food followed a more or less set pattern: cereal, fruit, and coffee for breakfast; a light sandwich lunch in the heat of the day; tea in the afternoon; and our main meal, consisting of stew, mashed potatoes, and coffee, at night.

Bread would not have kept, so we carried over two thousand Ryvitas. We both used to like Ryvita before that trip, but by the time we reached Barbados neither of us ever wanted to see, smell, or hear of one again.

Ever tried a slightly damp Ryvita and sardines?

The fresh fruit was lasting well. It was mainly citrus: oranges, lemons, and grapefruit that we had bought green in Las Palmas very cheaply and were eating as they ripened. Still, as a precaution, we were taking vitamin and ascorbic acid tablets every day. The ascorbic acid, by the way, is against scurvy, in place of the old-fashioned lime juice for which Limeys are famous.

We were fond of tinned fruit but it was expensive and a luxury, so we bought six tins and had one between us every five hundred miles as a treat; in between times we tried to vary the diet as much as possible without actually making ourselves sick.

Our stews became definitely lurid at times. We would start off one day with a Basic Stew, consisting of a tin of corned

Sopranino

beef, a tin of peas, and one onion. Then the next day we would throw in, maybe, a tin of baked beans, and the next perhaps a tin of spaghetti, and so we would go on until the fifth or sixth generation, by which time it was getting out of hand, and we would hurl the remains at the fishes.

'Lurid' is your word.

Then, for a change, we would try something new, such as Savoury Potatoes and Onions, covered in Tomato Soup, just to get a different taste.

Oddly enough, although we ate Basic Stew solidly (and I use that word advisedly) for a year, it was one of the things of which we did not tire. I mean we could still face it and look it in the eye.

As we went on the wind swung around from the north-east to due east. Our destination was somewhere between west and southwest, while the trades are supposed to blow from the northeast, so we decided that this was a slant and took advantage of it to get out to the westward, to put ourselves in a good position to run down on Barbados when the wind went back into the northeast again.

There was an awkward, confused sea at this stage, caused by a sea from the eastward running across an old swell from the northeast, which suggested that our slant theory was correct.

Since Colin had adjusted the spinnaker the ship was going faster and was drier, but the motion was even wilder. Colin began to feel sick again, while I seemed to have a mild attack of Canary Fever, with headaches and the usual attendant troubles.

As we used up our water we would keep the empty pots for checking against the water schedule daily at midday, then the old ones that were no longer serviceable would be ceremoniously flung overboard, while the good ones were stowed away in the lockers again, separate from the full ones. Meanwhile we churned on out to the westward.

On Saturday, January 19, the log came up to 702. We were now over a quarter of the way across. The trade winds on sunny days, which means most days, are so like the movies it isn't true. The sea is a wonderful deep blue and so clear that you can see the log spinner in the water over 75 feet away, while puffy little white clouds are dotted across a clear blue sky.

So evenly are the clouds spaced that the whole scene seems to take on a circular pattern with youself in the middle. The horizon is circular, with a ring of apparently dense white clouds above it, thinning out as they rise up in a great dome to a clear blue patch overhead.

Meanwhile we, alone in the midst of this majestic beauty, went ahead with our own mundane affairs—inspecting the fruit and throwing away the odd ones that were going bad, filling the stoves with fuel, and rigging a throw-out antenna up the mast to improve the range of the radio.

That evening there were great celebrations in our little cabin. A glass of sherry preceded a ceremonial supper of tomato soup, stew, tinned pineapple, and coffee, after which we lay back in our bunks, replete and content, listening to Saturday Night Theatre, coming in on the radio from England 2500 miles away, while our ship forged onwards across the wide ocean.

CHAPTER SEVEN

The Firgas Drinkers

Time Goes out of Joint—The Danger of Falling off—Sunshine and Showers—Clouds as Companions—The Barometer Drops—We Prepare for a Hurricane—Routines and Habits—Poetry and The Times*—Half-way—Celebrations—Partridge for Supper—Swimming a Thousand Miles from Land—Lights under the Water—The Long-Tailed Bird—Porridge Cakes—The Weather Is Tiresome—We Hold a Meeting*

EVEN if things went well, we could reckon that it would take us at least a month to cross the ocean, so now, with over two thousand miles of it ahead of us and no possibility of turning back, we began to settle down to our daily life alone out there on the face of the sea.

It is remarkable how well one does settle in in a tiny boat hundreds of miles from any land. Sitting in the hatch as the sun went down ahead of us, enjoying a quiet glass of red wine and a cigarette, we found life really very pleasant and certainly a fine relaxation after the weeks of hard work ashore.

The cigarette, by the way, was my second since we had left Las Palmas. It had taken ten days before we had got used to the wild motion of trade wind sailing to the point where I could smoke one without being sick. Colin never smoked anyway, regarding it as a heathen and rather revolting habit, so he could afford to sit and look smug about the whole business.

Planing, or rather surf-riding, had now become so frequent as to cause no comment, and sitting together in the cabin listening to the radio in the evening we were mildly annoyed when the roaring vibration of the fin interrupted the programme or when the fan of spray at the bow threw a few drops of water down the hatch.

When Sopranino *went surfing on the face of a breaking sea, her speed through the water was for a short time close to the speed of the crest, which must have been of the order of ten to fifteen knots. Our speed*

The Firgas Drinkers

relative to the wind dropped to a point where our sails became almost be-calmed. As they controlled the steering, it meant that we were without control when we got to the bottom, and so swung around sideways on to the next wave. This was of little importance, for we were so light that we were chucked clear of the breaking water and, as soon as we stopped, the breeze caught up with us, filling the sails, which promptly pulled the tiller over and off we went again.

Quite often *Sopranino* would be caught by a wave and swung right round. However, we were used to that by now, and it had become common to see Colin looking pained as he held his bowl of stew almost vertically on edge to prevent it from spilling.

With the increased speed we were making some fine days' runs; 119 miles was our best so far, but that is very nice going for a small one, when you realise that it is common for a large tanker with powerful engines to average only 200.

I will not have Sopranino *compared to a tanker.*

One morning when I was sitting cooking breakfast, the boat gave an unusually violent lurch, catching me unawares. As she went down, the lid of the kettle rose straight up on a neat round column of water which came splashing down boiling hot all over my bare legs.

A day or two of regular applications of vaseline soon put it right, but we had learned our lesson. From then on whenever we went below to cook, even in the heat of the tropical sun, we always spread an oilskin jacket over our knees to keep hot liquids off.

We wore our oilskins much more when down below than when we were on deck.

Boiling fat, of course, would have been very much worse, so any kind of frying was off, except in the very calmest weather. And so our diet settled down too. Stew and coffee, coffee and stew.

Don't you mean: Stew, Ryvita and Coffee; Cocoa, Ryvita, and Stew?

Usually the wind would hot up in the day time and ease off at night, but there was one night when it went the other way, getting even stronger. At about four in the morning we took out the stop watch and timed ourselves for over twelve seconds

Sopranino

on the face of one wave. Twelve seconds is a long time to spend hanging up there in the darkness with nothing underneath you, skimming along on the top of a breaker.

And as we went on out to the westward, time itself began to go haywire. The sun would rise and set later and later, until we had to put our cabin clock back another hour, the second since we left the Canary Islands.

In principle we took sight on the sun every third day to check our position, but if the sun happened to be obscured by a cloud, what the hell; tomorrow would do. There was nothing to hit for thousands of miles ahead.

On deck, whether working or just sun-bathing, we always wore a personal life-line—a length of strong rope around our waists and secured to the mast. Then if we should slip and fall overboard we would have a sporting chance of pulling ourselves in again. Anyway, we would at least stay with the boat, which is the first principle on the sea. To be alone out there with no boat would be a silly situation, to be avoided at all costs.

In fact if you were to fall off at night without a life-line you might just as well jump off the Empire State Building for all the chance you would have of living through it. By the time the other man realised that you were no longer around the boat would be miles away, and with the best will in the world the chances of his finding your head, bobbing around on that vast waste of water, would be negligible.

Always made a point of tying the life-line around the other man's waist for him, so that if you woke up to find yourself alone, it would be your own fault.

It was not always fine and sunny, though nearly so. But when the weather did change it changed very rapidly. One moment there would not be a cloud in the sky; then a tiny dark patch would appear on the horizon behind us, to windward. Within half an hour a great dirty rainsquall would be on top of us, washing the salt off us with a real tropical downpour driven by sharp little gusts of wind.

Then, half an hour later it would be gone. Rapidly everything would dry out, leaving no sign that it had ever been. To tell the truth we rather welcomed the coolness of these showers and it was only when they occurred just as we were about to take a sight, obscuring the sun and wasting all our preparation, that we were annoyed with them.

On Tuesday morning, January 22, as the dawn came up in many pastel shades of pink and cream the log revealed that we had passed the thousand mark. A thousand miles gone and some seventeen hundred to go. In fact, the log itself only went up to a hundred before it came around and started again, but we were deeply interested in that instrument, taking a careful note of what it had to say at least four times a day.

If it showed the slightest sign of going around more slowly than usual, we would attack it with soothing oils to keep the works at their best.

Already the moon was getting very small. When we had started out it had been round and full, lighting our way for us across the water ahead. Now it had waned away to a little semicircular splinter of light in the sky, but it was to wax large and bright again before we reached the other side.

Our pale dawn soon developed into a fine sunny morning, brisk and clear, with practically no clouds. Just one small sample of each type dotted around the horizon. Clouds had become an important part of our life. After all, where we were there was only the sea and the sky and us. The sea we used to float on, to wash things in, and to dispose of anything that we didn't want. The sun and the moon and the stars we used for navigation, to tell us where we were and which way to go next.

The clouds were to tell us about the weather that was coming, as well as to admire and enjoy. There are many different kinds of clouds and they all have names. Those dark grey rainclouds, low and ragged and menacing, are called nimbus, while the round white puffy clouds that look like lumps of cotton wool are cumulus. Then there are stratus—flat clouds that look as though they have been painted on the sky—and high up you will find cirrus and altus types, way at the top, looking like mares' tails and tiny white cabbages.

Sopranino

And then of course there are the in-betweens, clouds that couldn't make up their minds which they wanted to be. The most obvious of these is the cumulo-nimbus, a large grey nimbus type of cloud that has piled itself up the way a cumulus will, mounting way up into the sky and sometimes spreading out into a great anvil at the top. They are a particularly obnoxious breed that have a habit of tearing the wings off aircraft and the sails off the boats.

At sea the helmsman would keep an eye lifting to windward, to see what was coming. The low clouds that mean immediate trouble come down at you on the wind, and you can usually judge whether or not they are going to pass over you.

The cumulus are harmless enough unless they are large, when they may have a drop of wind in them. The nimbus look dark and fierce, but most likely they've got no more than a hatful of rain and a few sharp squalls for you. Rain itself is a discomfort, but only becomes a hazard when it cuts down the visibility.

Cumulo-nimbus want watching, though, for they will almost certainly have quite a bit of wind all around them. This is caused by the vast updraught of air in the middle which brings the surface winds rushing towards the base. In northern latitudes this takes the form of an anti-clockwise spiral so that as you watch them approaching you can estimate fairly accurately what the strength and direction of the wind will be when it comes.

Thunderclouds are the exception. They have a habit of developing to windward faster than the wind is moving, so that they will come creeping up on you from behind while you are looking the other way.

The high clouds, the altus and the cirrus, are so far up that they are out of the surface wind and will frequently be seen moving in quite a different direction, riding along on the high-altitude winds. These are the heralds that come to warn you of big storms approaching that may be days off yet.

All these things were of immediate daily importance to us out there on the ocean. From the signs in the sky we would decide to set another sail or take one in, or even what time we would have our next meal and what it should be.

One thing that became a fixed institution was our morning stare. Each in his turn would stand with his legs in the hatch and his arms over the boom, just staring, like a cow, at everything and nothing, for half an hour. A wonderful and satisfying occupation, far removed from the hustle and bustle of life ashore.

The morning stare was also an evening institution just before bedtime.

Not that there was not plenty to do. In effect we were on duty for twenty-four hours a day, ready at a second's notice to cope with anything that should turn up, and all the time conscious of everything that was going on—the state of the weather, the wind, the visibility, and the sea. Planning strategic manoeuvres such as taking advantage of a slant of wind and tactical manoeuvres like dodging a local storm kept us alert and watchful every minute of the day.

Hah! And planning practical manoeuvres like the finding of the second-last tin of fruit for the evening's celebration without having more than two objects loose at a time. One in each hand.

We had complete trust in each other's judgment; that was essential, so that if one was on watch the other would sleep soundly and in peace. But when we were both below the least change in the motion or the feel of the ship would send us scurrying on deck to see what was up.

Besides all this there were the everyday duties and chores to be done. Cooking, washing up, cleaning, mending, counting out stores, and checking, always checking, every little thing.

All the time the sea seemed to get bluer and clearer. We were told that it is so clear in Barbados that they cannot land flying boats there; they just can't tell where the surface is.

Quite often, we were going so fast that the decks were awash, but everything below was still nice and dry. The JOG rule that the hatch opening must be three inches above deck level was paying off. Time after time water would come swishing along the deck, but always it would stop at the hatch, to run off harmlessly into the sea.

Sopranino

Scrubbing the decks of Sopranino *was a gentlemanly occupation. First you wait for a day on which the seas wash over them. Then take off your shoes and climb on to the foredeck with a bottle or packet of detergent. Sprinkle the detergent on the deck. The next wave produces a lather and the next sweeps it clean. And there it is.*

We were getting rather more water in the bilges now, some-times as much as a quart a day. There were two theories about this: Colin thought it might be caused by leakage at the keel, due to the excessive strains on the fin; I thought it was the heat causing the exposed topsides to dry out a little and open up. We both hoped I was right, since that was far less serious, and as it turned out I was, for as soon as she got into the cool climates again she was as dry as ever.

Still don't agree. The topsides were washed all the time by sea water, which kept them cool enough, and anyway a month at moorings in the tropics did not seem to have any effect. On the other hand, the strain on the fin-keel must have been immense when it was vibrating. How-ever, when we examined her after the trip, there was no sign of paint cracking to indicate any movement whatsoever of the topsides or keel. Perhaps it was all the copper fastenings expanding in the heat.

Out on deck in the tropical sun it really was very hot. Colin would move around, trying to keep in the shade, while I sat like a mushroom, in my own private patch of shade under a great, floppy, girl's straw hat that I had bought in Las Palmas for the purpose. It must have been quite a sight from Colin's point of view: the floppy hat with ribbons on it and underneath a bronzed ocean voyager in dark glasses and bathing trunks, smoking a pipe.

Taking sights on the sun in a tiny boat in a seaway presents quite a problem. It is more a question of speed and skill than anything else, like shooting snipe from the back of a swaying camel. You only get a look at the horizon for a fleeting second as she comes up to the top of a wave. Then the crest catches her, swings her wildly, and the sun disappears out of your view through the telescope. To make things worse, just as you are getting ready for a shot she will roll, bringing the sail down to cut off the view.

The Firgas Drinkers

So we developed a system: Colin would keep the ship as steady as possible with one hand, manipulating a stop watch, paper, and pencil with the other, while I worked the sextant. I would take a series of six or eight shots, while Colin would record the exact time of each, to the nearest half-second. Then I would retire below and plot them all against time on graph paper, reject the duds, and select the most likely looking one to work our position from.

As a matter of interest I once set the sextant to an error equivalent to five miles and looked at the sun through it. The error was quite clear and obvious, so we reckoned that our sights were probably accurate to within two miles, which is quite good enough.

From the start we had been taking readings of all our instruments every six hours, at least, and recording them carefully in the ship's log book. Suddenly the barometer, which had been almost steady for a long time, dropped sharply. There were no signs of bad weather in the sky, but barometers don't drop for nothing. Something was cooking, and it could be a hurricane.

According to the rules, hurricanes should not happen in January, but we had been told that there might always be the spare one that didn't know about the rules, and hurricanes are not things to be trifled with at any time.

The book on hurricanes said definitely that if the barometer dropped five millibars, then a hurricane was certain. It was as we got to this that we looked up and noticed that our barometer had dropped just five millibars. Still, I was never very certain that our barometer had a fighting chance in life. It lived on the bulkhead at the foot of our bunks, at the greatest distance possible from the fresh air.

We went over in detail the drill that we had worked out for dealing with one if it came, and then retired below to read up all about their habits and the exact signs that would indicate each stage of the game. Colin put an extra lashing on the radio, just in case.

The weather was hot then, and rather oppressive, though we ourselves had been taking our vitamins and ascorbic acid daily and were now feeling fitter than when we had left Las Palmas. We did one silly thing. We opened up a skin of wine and took a sip each before we discovered that it had gone bad. Quickly we threw it overboard, hoping that there would be no ill effects.

In the middle of the night we ran through a rainsquall into a patch of flat calm. Now what was up? Perhaps we had gone too far to the north and run out of the trades, or perhaps the hurricane was closing in. The barometer was low but steady, which was a good sign. We sat and waited to see what would happen.

In the morning the wind was back in the east, but the sky was dark and grey with rainclouds as far as the eye could see in every direction, while sharp little squalls were passing over us all the time.

Then, quite suddenly, the whole thing passed over. The barometer rose a little, the sky cleared, and we were back to normal again, bowling along in the trade winds towards our destination. We both turned in for a good sleep.

Although we were over a thousand miles out now and far from any shipping lane, we still kept watch during the hours of darkness. One of us would be on duty from dusk until midnight and the other took over from then until dawn, sitting in the cabin, but putting his head out every now and then for a good look around to check that everything was all right and that the rare steamer had not come wandering up from South America or somewhere. Then as soon as it was fully light and our little boat was plainly visible on the face of the water, the duty watch would also turn in for a few hours' sleep.

That afternoon it was fine and sunny. Soon everything was dry after the morning's rain, the barometer was rising steadily, the decks were dry, and life was very pleasant once more.

We began to develop little habits as time went on. Colin liked his morning glass of lemonade, with a slice of lemon in it, served on the foredeck at eleven. Rotten tomatoes we disposed of by flinging them over the mast top, taking care not to let them lodge in the rigging. They fall later.

We got a fair amount of exercise from the very effort of

The Firgas Drinkers

continually bracing ourselves against the motion of the ship, but now and then we felt in need of a good stretch. So it was not uncommon to come up on deck and find one's partner standing on the stern of the boat, solemnly touching his toes or, perhaps, swinging on the boom like a monkey.

The oranges finished on the twelfth day out, mostly because they were very good and we ate them up, but the tomatoes, onions, and potatoes continued to last well, with very few going bad. The onions and potatoes began to sprout, but that did not seem to affect the taste; the tomatoes had to be sorted almost daily, to see that the bad ones did not affect the others.

We had two wet batteries for the lights and the first of these was still lasting well, long after we had passed the thousand-mile mark. (The radio had its own dry batteries.) True, we did not keep the lights burning all night out there, but we did quite a bit of reading in our bunks in the evenings and had light whenever we wanted it.

Apart from our one novel, *The Pursuit of Love*, that had been given us as we left, we had allowed ourselves one book each for the journey. Both of us had chosen poetry. Colin had *The Oxford Book of English Verse* while I chose *Other Men's Flowers*, an anthology of poetry collected by Lord Wavell.

It turned out to be an excellent policy, for it was remarkable how well the poetry lasted. In the first week we each read our novel through a couple of times, and that was that. But the books of poetry went on lasting and lasting, always giving us something fresh and new to think about until long after the voyage was over.

Once we had got used to the rolling it was surprising how little one noticed the movement down below in the cabin. Our reactions to it became quite automatic, until we ceased to be aware of it any more than one is aware of the ticking of a clock in a room at home. Everything was securely wedged in its right position, so that we lost all sense of any motion until we went out on deck.

There we were suddenly struck by all the movement going on, with the ship worming her way through the waves, the

Sopranino

spray flying, and the sea rushing past less than half an inch, through the sides of the ship, from the peace and quiet below.

We were both developing sore behinds, though, from sitting through the long night watches. We had long since compressed our cushion into a solid mass closely resembling a lump of concrete, and on this we would sit, hour after hour, braced with our knees against the locker, quietly packing it down still further.

Sometimes as I sat there in the cabin looking out through the windows at the sun glinting on the Atlantic Ocean I could not help remembering the days when I had sat in that same position, on that same seat, when *Sopranino* was being built in the shed at Woottens; or the time when I had stood with Giles, the designer, looking at a series of chalk lines on a bare floor, and had turned to ask him how he thought she would go in the trade winds.

Then he had said nothing, just giving me an amused smile, but now we were in it, well over a thousand miles in it, for better or for worse.

Time out there seems to stand still, or rather to repeat itself like a tune on a cracked gramophone record. The sun rises out of the sea behind you, passes overhead, and disappears below the horizon ahead. Then the moon and all the stars come out, slowly swinging across the sky in great arcs, until the sun puts its head over the edge of the world once more and they fade and flee like ghosts of the night.

Each day one rises, eats, works, and sleeps. And the next day the same, and the next and the next. *Small* time there is, yes, between breakfast and lunch or lunch and supper, but *big* time—days, weeks, months—no. In fact it seemed all the time that it was only yesterday or the day before that we had said goodbye to Kenny and started out.

Just after dark the news would come in well on the radio from the BBC in London, then it would go patchy; later on, the long wave would come breaking through, bringing us plays and entertainment for the evenings.

Then, late at night, after Colin was asleep, I would be sitting in the hatch writing up the log book when Splash! down would come a dollop of spray, soaking the book and me too, just to remind me that the sea was all around us still.

Whenever we were going fast, around five knots or more, the motion would be rather jumpy, with wet decks and the occasional slop of spray down the hatch, but when the wind eased off a little and our speed fell to four knots the decks would be dry, the motion easier, and all would be calm and peaceful.

On Friday, January 25, just two weeks out from Las Palmas, we reached the half-way mark. Halfway; 1400 sea miles behind us and 1400 more ahead. Running down our westing in the trade winds as the ancient mariners had done before us. Seeing the same sights, hearing the same sounds as Columbus and his men had seen and heard.

Exactly the same, for the sea does not change. Man may dig down into the earth for rock and pile it up into buildings and monuments that may last for thousands of years after his time, but let him pass across the sea, even fight grim battles on it in his mightiest warships, and when he has finished it will still be the same, timeless and relentless, showing no sign that he has ever passed that way.

And now I really must go and wash my socks, for this was a great day. At lunch-time we opened our latest copy of *The Times* Weekly Edition, reading it through carefully from top to bottom and corner to corner, page by page. Just before we had left Las Palmas we had been given four copies of *The Times*, one for each week. True they were a month old, but we had not read them so what was the difference? The news was still as bad as ever. And now, every Friday, we would open the latest copy and see what was new since last week.

We checked our water schedule. We were well ahead, leaving ourselves with plenty to spare for a bath and even washing our clothes. Then we checked our food stores; they were going well, too, so we brought out further supplies from the main storage lockers on each side of the cockpit and stowed them for ready use under the galley and chart table.

Amongst them we found a tin of partridge, so that evening

Sopranino

we had a very special supper: tomato soup, partridge, peas, tomatoes, mashed potatoes, apricots, and coffee, rounded off with the last of the sherry and a couple of cigarettes. Then we both lay back in our bunks, full and torpid, and fell asleep.

About half-past three in the morning I woke up, for no apparent reason, and stuck my head out of the hatch. There, about a mile away, passing us, was a large ship shinning across the water in a blaze of light. Rumbling and splashing its way over the sea. That was the first ship that we had sighted; the first sign of civilisation that we had seen since the fifteenth, eleven days ago.

I called Colin out on deck and together we stood and stared at it as it went by, thinking of all those people asleep in their bunks, who in a few days' time would be ashore in some strange land while we would still be out there on the ocean, living our lives the same as before.

We did flash our lantern at it in the hope of getting it to send a message home to say that we were all right, but there was no reply. It never saw us. We hardly expected that it would, for the look-outs would not be searching the horizon for tiny boats out there nearly a thousand miles from anywhere.

And so we stood in silence, watching it go, until it dwindled to a point of light and disappeared. At that rate the next one was not due for a couple of weeks and meanwhile we might as well get some sleep, so we both turned in again.

Once or twice we were woken up by a strange knocking noise. *Bonk*. Then a long silence. Then *Bonk* again. Or *Bonk*, *Bonk*. It was mystifying. We checked everything. No, it wasn't inside. We looked outside, but there was nothing there, nothing but sea and more sea, wide and deep. Finally we decided it must be Davy Jones, come to claim us, so back we went to sleep again.

In the morning it was clear and sunny and cheerful. The wind had eased a little and the rough tops had vanished from the waves, smoothing them off into a series of nice, even curves that left us very comfortable and dry.

It was a day for doing pleasant things. Washing, drying,

The Firgas Drinkers

sun-bathing, and taking photos. We were now over a thousand miles from any land in any direction, in water over fifteen thousand feet deep, so I took a whole series of photos, more than a hundred, illustrating all phases of life out there.

Obviously we must have a swim a thousand miles from anywhere, so down came the sails as we stopped the ship. As soon as we stopped moving the wind began to hum in the rigging, for although it was a quiet day by trade wind standards it was still blowing quite strongly, and of course if we had started going against it it would have become a good deal stronger.

Next we joined together all the spare ropes that we could lay our hands on to make one long line, tied an inflated fender to the end of it, and let it out behind us. Something to grab on to if the ship should move off and leave us behind.

Then we took it in turns to stand guard, keeping a way eye out for sharks, while the other had his swim. It was nice to splash around free in the water, knowing that there was an awful lot of it around, and to see our boat as the fishes saw it, drifting silently overhead; but personally I kept wondering just what lived out there in the depths of the sea and was quite glad to scramble back on board again.

It was worth going for a swim, if only to have a look at Sopranino. *It is perhaps the greatest pity in sailing that you so seldom see your own boat at sea. One day I am going to have two boats exactly the same. I shall sail in one and look at the other, to extract the last ounce of pleasure. And if it happens that I cannot have two lovely boats, and I become bitter, I shall sail around in the ugliest of boats that I can find, looking at everyone else's nice boat, while they have to avert their gaze from mine.*

While we were bathing a flying fish, *Sopranino*-size, came aboard. It was about an inch and a half long, with long thin wings like a dragonfly's. How it managed to fly that high we never knew, but it was duly photographed along with the rest of us.

A lovely afternoon with perfect trade wind clouds, round little cumulus clouds that might have had an angel sitting on each one, spaced as evenly as cabbages in a field as far as the eye could see in every direction. Then a Technicolor sunset, and down below to listen to the BBC saying that it had been freezing all day in England, with snow and ice on the roads all over the country.

The BBC was still coming through quite nicely, though Brazil was now our nearest and loudest station, very jolly if only we could understand it, and every now and then we would get the United States.

San Juan, Puerto Rico, was also loud in our cabin.

We checked our chronometer against the time signals. It was gaining $7\frac{1}{2}$ seconds a day. Since we had left England its rate had gone up from $5\frac{1}{2}$ to $6\frac{1}{2}$ and now $7\frac{1}{2}$ seconds a day. That was not too bad. So long as we knew what it was gaining and it remained steady, then we could navigate by it all right. It is when they start gaining one day and losing the next that you never know where the devil you are.

Probably the increase was due to the steady rise in average temperature. It was supposed to be compensated for temperature, but possibly not for that much temperature. Anyhow it was behaving itself, so all was well.

And we found out what that knocking was. It was not Davy Jones after all, but the port guy block, gently lifting off the deck as the sail pulled the line tight and then dropping back with a *bonk* when the wind eased for a moment. Colin studied it for a while, then overcame the whole problem by the delightfully simple expedient of fixing a piece of soft rubber for it to land on.

Although we were now over a thousand miles from the nearest land in any direction, there was no sensation of loneliness or of being particularly far from land, and the sea generally was much the same as it is anywhere else.

That was a fantastic evening. A calm gentle swell, with a brilliant starry sky and a warm gentle breeze. Standing in the hatch after supper as *Sopranino* steered herself towards the West Indies, with light and music coming faintly from the cabin, I was very conscious of that tiny little box of civilisation gliding silently across the ocean. That is the kind of moment we go sailing for.

The Firgas Drinkers

Now the stars were so bright that they made lanes of shimmering light, radiating across the water all around us like the spokes of a giant wheel. Definitely a night to remember for a lifetime.

Little things—radio, electric light, shaving, and the occasional drink—make life very civilised. Also poetry and *The Times* and our morning lemonade in the sun.

Colin had rigged up a cunning little light out of an old bicycle rear lamp, run by a used radio battery. It gave us enough light to see what we were doing and saved the main batteries. It was lasting very well and he said he found it less sick-making than the full-powered ones.

The last few nights Colin had been complaining of lights, like 100-watt bulbs, passing by about six feet down in the water. Idly I wondered whether it was indigestion or brandy.

Indigestion or brandy it may have been, but you saw them yourself next night.

Although we were both sleeping these nights, any time that we happened to wake up we would go out on deck for a while, to admire the view and have a look around. Once or twice on these occasions we would get all excited over a single white light low on the horizon that looked just like an approaching steamer, but each time it would turn out to be a rising star.

Stars rising out of the sea are most deceptive, but the moon rising through a cloud is worse. Coming back to England in the yawl Bloodhound, *I all but turned out the watch below for what I was convinced was an ocean liner about to run us down until, just as it was upon us, it rose out of the sea altogether.*

The next morning was as magnificent as the evening before. Just nicely cool, with a few clouds on the horizon to the north and a few to the south and the sun shining like a white hot disk out of a clear pale-blue sky, throwing a path of burnished silver towards us across the slightly purple face of the blue sea.

Later on quite a bit of high cloud developed, almost as if there was a storm approaching from the south. We watched and wondered and waited. Meanwhile our second flying fish came aboard, an inch long this time but a good specimen, with well-developed wings. We put it in the sun to dry but it promptly burst. Then a white bird with a very long tail, possibly a bo'sun bird, came flying over. It felt like visiting day.

We had not been able to get any detail charts of the approaches to Barbados. We had one chart of the whole ocean; then the next was a large one of the island itself. So to check our course as we ran in on the island I prepared a set of three home-made ones, each twice the scale of the next, on which I should be able to plot our position and check our exact drift in those vital last few days.

The last of the tomatoes were beginning to go bad all at once. We managed to save eleven of them and then cast the crate overboard to find its own way across the ocean. Probably it has reached the island by now.

For a few minutes the wind dropped right away, for the second time since we were in the trades, but it soon came back again, though less strongly than before. I took the opportunity, while the sea was relatively calm, to make some experiments in the galley.

The serious things that we had run out of so far were sweets and cakes. We used more of these than I had allowed for, since each time a man went on watch he would take a few cakes and a few sweets with him: something to chew when one was alone with the sea.

On the other hand we had a surplus of sugar, porridge oats, condensed milk, and cooking oil. Obviously, then, the thing to do was to find a way of making cakes out of these things. So I made little ones of condensed milk and porridge, about the size of half-a-crown but thicker, coated them with sugar, and fried them in oil.

The results were interesting. Colin, a true Scot, was of course scandalised by the whole business, desecrating the good name of porridge, but personally I thought that they were all right, and they were something to chew.

Not that I would pour scorn on your porridge cakes. They really were wonderful . . . and I don't know how you managed to eat so many.

The answer to the whole problem, of course, would be to

have all the cakes made up in sealed containers at the start, marked for opening at specified days or mileages but, for the moment, we had porridge cakes.

That night another little calm left us rolling and still for five minutes, with our sails flapping to and fro as we rolled. I came out to see what all the fuss was about and there, beside us, was a luminous object about the size of a cabbage, drifting quietly by some three feet down in the water. Whatever it was I suppose it lives in those parts.

For a few nights there was no moon at all, which left the sky clear for the millions of stars to wink and shine their best. From the point of view of navigation, Orion turned out to be very reliable, always turning up where it should be when it was wanted, but the Pole Star was no good at all as it was by then so low on the horizon that it was almost always obscured by the clouds.

Sometimes small local rainstorms would come drifting by us, one or two dark nimbus clouds often passing quite close, with the rain clearly visible underneath them so that we could see it striking the water while we sat in the sunshine watching.

Although neither of us is routine-minded we found that we fell into a routine of life by which one of us rose about 7.30, dried out the bilges, washed up, cleaned up, and served breakfast to the other in his bunk around 9.30. He would then wash up again and serve lemonade at 11.00, lunch about 2.00, and cocoa around 5.00.

One more wash up and he would peel the potatoes and then hand over to the other, who would serve supper about 9.00 and take over the chores next morning. Also the one who served supper would be on duty and responsible for the ship, from 10 p.m. until 2 a.m., while the other one would be on from 2.00 until 6.00.

As things were going this arrangement worked very smoothly, giving us alternate days of chores and leisure. This, together with the navigation every three days and celebrations every five hundred miles, served to break up any tendency that there might have been for the thing to become monotonous.

Sopranino

Not counting, of course, the celebrations at the cardinal points, such as halfway and the quarters. Also, you forgot to say that we measured our 500 miles from both ends and we were on a passage of 2800 miles. We kept pretty busy. A celebration consisted of a glass of sherry at dinner-time. When the sherry ran out we had a brandy and soda, which again shows the forethought necessary for this kind of voyage. The Firgas made admirable soda.

For the next couple of days we had the impression that we were passing through strata of weather arranged laterally across our path. There would be little bits of everything—calms, rainstorms, thunderstorms—with winds blowing every way; then the trade winds would come back for a while, until we hit the next patch of storms.

We could not be bothered to keep rushing out on deck to reset the sails each time the wind changed, particularly as it was usually raining, so we just let her go and wandered around in circles as the storms passed over us. We were bored with the outside world for the moment so we just stayed in the cabin and ignored it, looking at the spare compass in disgust from time to time as we went round and round.

We found plenty to do, though, learning Spanish, doing chores, and cooking up vast supplies of porridge cakes. The sea itself didn't know what to think about it all either, for no sooner had it started running one way than the wind would blow from a different quarter, until we had three or four lots of waves running against and across each other, sometimes flattening each other out but more often piling up together into odd-shaped pyramids of water. The motion was jumpy and irregular, making life tiresome below. Even if your stew pot was only half-filled you had to sit there all the time it was cooking, holding the lid firmly down with a wet rag, to keep it from all jumping out.

Now, when I cooked stew I had to wedge the lid on with a prop to the deck above, even in the calmest of seas. I am deeply suspicious that it was the explosive mixture inside, rather than any outside force at work.

Even to write up the log book I found it necessary to lie on my back in my bunk with my feet on the ceiling and a torch

The Firgas Drinkers

wedged under my chin, and in the middle of the thunderstorms, when the rain was really teeming down, there would be the odd drip that would work its way cunningly along a beam and drop right down my neck.

A thunderstorm at sea in a small boat is quite an experience in itself. There you sit, alone on the face of the water, while the lightning comes crashing down all around you. And there is only one thing sticking up for miles and miles around . . . your mast, with its steel rigging pointing upward like a cone into the sky. There is nothing that you can do about it. You just sit and hope that the Good Lord will be kind and you won't be hit. That is a time when the poetry comes in handy. You can concentrate on trying to learn something by heart and forget all about the beastliness that is going on outside.

For, no matter how long and how carefully you may prepare, there are bound to be times when you will come up against forces beyond the control of man. When you have done all you can do, and must stand aside, as it were, trusting in the Good Lord to do as He sees fit.

On Tuesday, January 29, the weather sorted itself out and the log came up to 1700. Only a thousand miles to go. We pickled two of our onions in vinegar to make something new to eat and held another celebration. The night was fine—calm and clear once more, with warm soft breezes, a smooth sea, and a clear starry sky. A truly delightful evening altogether. Only that day I had been wondering how soon we would reach Barbados, but now I found myself thinking how lucky we were to have nearly a thousand miles of this fine sailing still ahead of us. The trade wind passage across the Atlantic must be one of the finest sails there is.

I took the sextant out and checked it on a star. No errors. Good! The new moon had come up now, shining clear and bright almost dead ahead of us. I took a sight on it for practice and to use as a check against our sun sights. It came out within a couple of miles of our calculated position, thereby increasing still further our confidence in this astro-navigation business.

The winds were still much more east than north. Our north-

Sopranino

westerly slant that we had been waiting for never came, so we braced around our sails and began cutting down more to the southward, towards the latitude of Barbados.

Less than a thousand miles to go. At last we had left the Cape Verde Islands behind and were well over on the western side of the ocean, churning along as before, surf-riding occasionally on the face of a wave, chipping those miles off one by one, day after day and night after night. Every day the sea is different and always it is more attractive.

Out in the cockpit we had put four large cans full of water as a reserve. Suddenly there was a quiet bump and a fountain of water, that we had carried and cherished for thousands of miles, going to waste. But, truth to tell, we had only lost half a gallon or so and we had plenty left. However, it did bring home the importance of carrying one's water in a series of small containers rather than in one big one which, if it burst, might lose you the lot. It must have been the expansion of the water in the sun that did it, so we opened up the others to let the pressure out of them before screwing the caps firmly down again.

Looking over the stern we found barnacles clinging to the transom, half-a-dozen little black fellows hanging on just above the water-line. They must have had a hard time, for the following seas had already knocked most of the paint off. But then they are a hardy lot. They will even cling to the log line, spinning around day and night without ever seeming to get dizzy.

Sometimes the clouds, particularly the cumulus variety, would pile themselves up into vast high masses, until they looked like the scenery for an Italian play. Colin, who paints, complained bitterly:

'You know, if I were to paint those things as they are, I should be told I wasn't telling the truth. There just aren't such clouds.' With which he resolutely turned his back on them.

Trade wind clouds at sunset are at times just too much. Great masses of reds, purples, and greens, piled in the most vulgar ostentation.

Out came the dry shaver and we gave each other a haircut with it. We kept a smart ship. It was part of our policy of

The Firgas Drinkers

demonstrating that not only could this sort of thing be done in such a tiny boat, but that it could be done efficiently and well.

Meanwhile, every now and then, we would sail through patches of what appeared to be vegetable matter floating on the surface of the water. It did not look as we had imagined plankton should. It was all very strange. Maybe it was edible, but it certainly did not look particularly appetising.

And ships discharge their waste tanks at sea.

By now I found that I could smoke up to four or five cigarettes a day without any sign of nausea, though somehow, out there, far from the rush and nervous strain of city life, one no longer felt the need to smoke. It was a pleasant thing to enjoy after a meal, but not a vital necessity as it sometimes is when one is worried and rushed ashore.

Before we had left England we had formed a small Partnership, with the idea of setting up an organisation to promote the sale of British boats and equipment in the United States, particularly the smaller types, and to make use of our own experience by bringing smaller, safer, and cheaper cruising boats to more and more people.

Now, after supper, we retired on deck, leaned over the boom, and held a Directors' Meeting in the tropical moonlight, discussing plans for operating in America and various kinds of craft. The meeting was finally closed by a rainstorm that sent us hurrying below again.

But it did not last long. They never do. And before we turned in the moon was once more shining bright and bold ahead of us, with a bright lone star beneath it, throwing a wide lane of ruffled silver light across the water, while in the gaps between the clouds we could identify the various stars that we should be needing for our run in to Barbados. Back in Las Palmas the local newspaper had called *Sopranino* 'The Smallest Ship in the World'. We were well on the way to proving them right.

I went below, but came out again. Something was wrong. The motion had changed. I checked the course on the compass. We were going southwest, towards South America. I

J   129

took a torch and had a look around. The rain had tightened the check lines on the tiller, locking the steering solid. Freed, the ship resumed her course once more.

With about eight hundred miles to go there was a definite feeling of 'running in' in the air, and excitement as we thought of seeing the West Indies, mixed with a sadness and nostalgia for our nice sail that so soon would be over.

CHAPTER EIGHT

Barbados

In the Tropics—Chasing Rattles—Running in—Planning Our First Meal Ashore-
Becalmed Seven Hundred Miles Offshore—Our Aiming Point—Flying Fish—One
Steamer, One Shark—Final Approach—Singing—We Sight Barbados Ahead—In
Port, but We Don't Go Ashore—Transatlantic Mail—Aboard H.M.S. Devonshire
for a Scrub

Friday, February 1. 0300. A fine clear night with just a little cloud round the
horizon. Otherwise the sky is clear and all the stars are plainly visible. It is
interesting to compare the sky now with last evening. Now the whole
heavens have gone round like the revolving stage in a theatre. Orion has
vanished, probably ahead, behind the sails, and many new stars have come
into view. The Plough is clearly visible to the northward and the Pole Star
itself is shining away there bright and clear. The ship is steering herself
nicely on course, bowling along before a warm gentle tropical night breeze
that hardly ruffles the surface of the water.

I WAS sitting in the hatch, writing up my notes in the log
book by flashlight, so as not to wake Colin, though sometimes I wondered just what would come nosing up out of the
depths of the ocean after the light one of those nights. Another
light bulb had just gone by in the water, about a 60-watter,
this time.

At three in the morning I was sitting there with no clothes
on except a thin pair of pants, and it was just nicely cool. It
was a truly remarkable night and a pity to go to bed. We had
had so much sleep lately that I was not tired at all. Still, I had
better turn in as I was on duty in the morning.

Just as I climbed into my bunk there was a rattle. 'Bother',
I thought. 'I must go and fix that.'

Rattles mean chafe and chafe means wear, so we spent much
of our lives chasing rattles. By then we could tell exactly what
any noise was as soon as it started, where it was, and what it
was doing. We had become such connoisseurs of extraneous
noise that we could even distinguish between the noise of a
Bovril pot and that of a Marmite pot in the same locker.

Sopranino

I glanced at the barometer. It had dropped again. Those drops, together with rises in temperature, were not very encouraging when one read the pilot book on the subject of hurricanes, but such is life at sea.

In the morning, as soon as the sun came up it would be hot on one's back, like standing too close to an electric fire. Now we really were in the tropics. When I was on duty, Colin would lie in his bunk, reading *The Times* and waiting for me to cook him his breakfast. But first I must go out and inspect the lemon.

Our last lemon was sunning itself in a corner on deck. We cherished that fruit, turning it round every few hours to make sure that it ripened evenly and became a succulent and delectable lemon.

With barely seven hundred miles to go there was much speculation about our arrival. We began working out in detail exactly what we would do when first we stepped ashore, planning our first meal, down to the last ice cream. Then we sharpened our blue pencil and spent an enjoyable afternoon plotting our proposed course through all the islands to the United States.

We still had forty pots of water left, enough for twenty days, but our meals were becoming dull and similar. We had hoped to have a tin of fruit that night, to celebrate the passing of two thousand miles, but the wind fell lighter and lighter and we did not quite make it.

Next morning when we woke up it was so still that we might have been in harbour. We had made the two thousand all right, but now the wind had left us completely, becalmed in the Antlantic Ocean seven hundred miles from the nearest island, Barbados.

All that day we lay there, hot and still. So still that we would throw our empty tins overboard after breakfast and they would still be right there beside us at lunch time. The water was deep-blue and very clear. Looking over the side we saw something weird and white beneath us. It was our own tea towel that we had been trailing behind us on a line to clean. Now, seventy feet or more down in the water, every detail of it could be made out.

Barbados

Our white, long-tailed water bird came over to visit us. We must have been the only feature on the horizon for hundreds of miles for him to visit on his morning fly. It was very much hotter now, with no breeze to cool us. The cabin was almost uninhabitable around midday and we were using appreciably more water than usual.

This was all very well if it didn't last too long. If it did, and our water ran out, things might be serious. Meanwhile we sat and we rattled, the sails flopping idly from side to side as we rolled on the remains of the swell with no wind to steady us.

This afternoon, note it well, Patrick went over the side for a swim. The first for six hundred miles.

But by nightfall even the swell had died down, leaving us silent and still in a still, silent world.

The following day was even flatter and calmer. The sea was as smooth as a gigantic sheet of glass, with microscopic shrimp-like creatures, plankton, in thousands of different varieties all over its surface. We stuck a knife in the mast and threw a penny overboard, two old seaman's dodges for raising wind, then sat back to await results.

Three dark-grey fish about a foot long and one tiny striped one that we promptly named Tiger Tim came over to stare at us and we, having nothing better to do, stared right back at them. Then we fed them on porridge and Ryvita and photographed them from all angles. Poor fish. Now they knew what it felt like to be Ocean Voyagers.

Soon we collected quite a variety of all sizes and shapes of fish around us. Quite tame, they would come up and nibble the food off our plates and fingers as we washed up over the side. Then a little breeze came up and we moved off across the water, our fish keeping their chosen stations around us in the hope of more delicacies.

We caught one by mistake. We had a line out astern with a hook on it; not that we really wanted to catch anything, but one is supposed to do these things, though why one should rush around killing things I never could appreciate. Anyway, there it was, way out astern, and we had forgotten it.

133

Sopranino

Then up came one of our fish friends with the hook in his mouth, looking sad and foolish, the line trailing in a long loop in the water behind him. We tried to get the hook out and release him, feeding him cheese to keep him happy while we did so, but no luck. It wouldn't come out, so we had to kill him. And having killed him we thought we'd better justify our actions by eating him. But we were very sad and he was very tough and one way and another we were nauseated by the whole business.

It was very sad indeed, for we had known him all day. We found out later, when we showed a sketch of him to the Bajians, that he was a type of fish known as an Old Wife, whose principal use to the world is that its skin is prized for scrubbing decks.

But we had learned one thing. We were not for fishing. We took the fishing line and stowed it away, deep down in the darkest locker where we could forget it. Meanwhile the breeze was developing nicely and we were really under way again. Already the wavelets were about a foot high, increasing all the time. We made our last lemon into lemonade and drank it by way of celebration.

It was very pleasant to be moving once more, with a breeze to keep us cool. Now we did not feel nearly so thirsty. We cut down to the southwest for a while, to dodge the rest of the calm patch if it was still about. This put us in the shade of the sails, which was a joy.

It is interesting to note that the great calm had all the characteristics of a 'High', while the barometer seemed to think it was a 'Low'. Odd.

All afternoon Colin kept seeing flying fish. No comment.

Nothing but ribald comments when I reported flying fish. We had to sail a day closer to them before Patrick would agree that he could see them himself. I think he was expecting small whales, or at least small sharks, passing overhead like Zeppelins.

Soon the waves were up to six feet high and we were doing little rushes down them, swinging around and broaching to with a wild jerk at the bottom. Back to normal; how nice.

Most of our fish had left us but Tiger Tim was still following in our wake, close under our stern, not seeming to mind being rolled over and over in the froth behind us.

That evening we sat on deck as the sun went down, full of the joy of being alive and afloat, admiring the clouds as they changed from gold to moonlit silver and thinking how wonderful it was to be out there, alone on the ocean, where one could appreciate these things. Then down below to supper, with the stove roaring away, leaving the ship to forge on through the night.

We had decided to make for a point three hundred miles east of Barbados and run in on the latitude of the north point of the island. There were several reasons for this. First of all, if by any chance the chronometer had gone haywire, which was most unlikely, we should still hit the island, though not exactly when we expected to, for our latitude would still be accurate while our longitude might be in error.

Then there would be a current, or drift, towards the northeast, around the island. That we knew, but not exactly in what direction or how strong, for it varies all the time with the condition of the wind and sea. By running in from due east we would be able to check this and make proper allowances for it. And lastly, we were having fun, besides following our established policy that you can't be too careful.

Soon we had less than five hundred miles to go and were less than two hundred from our aiming point. From there onward we should have to steer and keep watch for possible steamers, so we made the most of our last few nights of uninterrupted sleep.

We checked our food and water. We still had fourteen days' water and food for about a week at the standard rate, plus Ryvita, soup, and porridge for the Lord knows how long. Plenty, as long as we did hit the island. It was only about fifteen miles long by nine wide, alone in the ocean and more than a hundred miles from the next one. We would have come nearly three thousand miles without seeing land and had learned our navigation on the way. If we missed Barbados, then we might land up in Panama or anywhere. We had better not miss, that was all.

Sopranino

There really were flying fish now, hundreds of them, coming out of the water sometimes singly, sometimes in great schools, flying a hundred yards or more, perhaps ten feet above the crests of the waves, before they dived down in again. They varied in size, up to the size of a large herring, and had long, thin wings, nearly as long as their bodies, that folded flat beside them when they were in the water.

Nothing larger than a sardine ever landed on our decks, however we might think of them as a change for breakfast.

A small shark about five or six feet long followed us for a while, hoping that one of us would fall overboard. When we didn't, he took hold of the rotator on the end of our log line and pulled the line tight for a second. Then he got bored with that and sheered off.

Meanwhile we sat with a loaded pistol handy in case he got rough, and spent a happy afternoon discussing fine foods, occasionally staring hopefully ahead for signs of land. Just after dark a steamer, probably a tanker, passed across our bow about three-quarters of a mile away. Our second in a month. We put on our lights, but I don't think he noticed us.

On Wednesday, February 6, we hit our latitude with about 350 miles to go, and turned to the westward to run in, resetting our sails for the new course and throwing the last lime-juice bottle over. Now we had nothing left to drink except brandy and soda or whisky and soda. A hard life.

Patrick, who occasionally has a complicated turn of mind, spent his spare time calculating average speeds to be maintained for the sighting of Barbados at every hour of every day. When he got around to the higher speeds he started singing. I brewed him a hasty cup of coffee.

On the new course we were able to set an extra sail and with the ship lightened of most of the stores we were going really fast, the tiller trembling all the time as the rudder vibrated in the water rushing past it. Below, it was very steady after all the rolling of the last three weeks, and outside a large seagull and many small flying fish played around us, and Colin sang. No comment.

Barbados

And of course, with the hand-steering which we had re-started, we were usually able to stop her broaching round at the end of a period of surfing. Without the delay of waiting for the wind to put her back on course, we were surfing much more often. Once we surfed on six successive waves. Our average speed rose and we made our best day's run of 134 miles.

Suddenly Colin burst out laughing, bringing me on deck to see what it was all about. We were planing, rushing over the waves, leaving two trails of white stretching far out on the water behind us.

As we approached our aiming point we had begun to check our position more and more frequently. Now as we ran in to Barbados we took a sight each day to check the drift, so that we could correct our course for it before we got there. The only trouble was that I had lost one of the vital pieces of paper that I needed for working out the answers, and could not find it anywhere. There was only one solution: I should have to work from memory and hope for the best.

We kept calculating how far we had to go to Barbados. Thursday's run was fast, 130 miles in the twenty-four hours, bringing it down to less than 220, and by midday on Friday the log was reading 2575. Ninety-eight miles to go, if our calculations were correct.

There are three lighthouses on the eastern side of the island. One on North Point, one at the south, and one on Ragged Point that stands out to seaward somewhere in the middle. We were aiming for North Point, but at night we might see Ragged Point first, though it should be away over to our left.

On Friday I calculated that we were about five miles north of track, steering a little to the south. If we stayed on the same course we should see the lighthouses about three or four in the morning.

I tried for a radio bearing, but Barbados is one of those stations that only comes on when you call for it, and we had no transmitter to call for it with, so on we went, keeping a sharp look-out ahead, hoping and wondering.

It rained all afternoon, cutting down the visibility, but

137

Sopranino

cleared in the evening for a fine night, though the brilliant moon still made it difficult to see ahead.

At two in the morning we had supper, staring all the time expectantly ahead, though we were not quite due there yet. At three we saw a light, but it turned out to be a steamer. Still, it was a good sign.

At 4.30 a light winked on the horizon, over to port. It should be Ragged Point. We carried on. And at five up came North Point light, dead ahead. I was on watch alone; Colin had been asleep since supper and had missed all this, but as navigator I wasn't going to call him until I was quite sure we'd hit the right place.

As it got light I could make out the island. Ragged Point over to my left, then green fields and low hills sweeping round to North Point ahead. That was it, all right! I could contain myself no longer. Proudly I called Colin to come and look at my new Island I'd found.

He stuck a tousled head out of the hatch, glared at the thing with distaste, muttered something and went back to bed, leaving me alone with my thoughts.

Slowly the sun rose out of the sea in a blaze of gold, developing the scene around us. Ahead the sky paled to a brilliant blue and threw the clouds into sharp relief as they changed from pink to white. All around the deep-blue Atlantic rollers followed each other in even lines, ruled by the trade winds from infinity to infinity, every now and then breaking in a smother of white foam.

In the middle, our little boat rose and fell and wound and swung, racing down the faces of the seas, spray flying out on either side as her white sails strained and pulled her to the westward.

And out ahead, there it lay—Barbados, wonderfully green after so many weeks of blue. We had the answer to one more question. Little boats like ours could take their oceans as they took their seas, in their stride.

By eight o'clock we were swinging round North Point into the calm water behind the island, 29 days and 2700 miles out

Barbados

of Las Palmas, to heave to in Maycock's Bay. There we lay in pale-green water, flat calm and so clear that we could see the bottom a half mile from the shore. We cleaned and tidied the boat, washed and shaved ourselves, washed our hair and changed into our best whites so that we could arrive in Bridgetown Harbour looking smart and tidy.

As we lay there the local bus, a native schooner that runs twice daily from one end of the island to the other, passed by, laden down with everything from passengers to goats.

After breakfast we sailed slowly down the sheltered side of the island, taking in all the details on the shore—fields, trees, houses, and the green hills behind—while the warm earthy smells floated across the water to us. We rounded the last little headland into Carlisle Bay, where two warships and half-a-dozen merchantmen were lying to their anchors in the smooth water. Bridgetown itself stretched round in a great curve towards the Yacht Club on the far side where a number of small boats were moored.

As we sailed across the bay we noticed that all the ships had their ensigns at half-mast. We had not heard the news for several days but we feared that we knew what it meant. King George VI had died a few days before and all the town was in mourning for the passing of a great and selfless person. We dipped our own small ensign in salute and went over to the Yacht Club to report our arrival.

We couldn't go ashore until the health and customs authorities had cleared us and we had no anchor since ours had been stolen in Las Palmas, so we sailed across to the largest yacht in the harbour and asked if we might tie on behind her for a while.

Her owner threw us a line, and we bobbed on the water behind her like a dinghy. Nobody could come in contact with us until we had been cleared for health, so she let out her own dinghy, full of good food and drinks, on a long line to us. We had arrived.

She had watched our arrival through binoculars, and had remarked: '*Oh, they can't have come from anywhere. They are much too clean.*'

It was Saturday afternoon and soon the editor of the local

Sopranino

newspaper came over in his sailing boat to take our story, sailing around us as he did so; then one by one more boats collected around us as we sat, eating our food and drinking our drinks and enjoying doing nothing but chatter to all these new people.

Later on the customs and health officers came over and cleared us, but we were in no hurry to go ashore now. It was there when we wanted it and meanwhile we were content to sit and admire it from a distance.

When we did go ashore, on Monday, we delivered our one piece of mail, a letter from Mrs Staib in Las Palmas to her mother in Barbados, with a photograph of the new baby that she had never seen. As a matter of fact we forgot to put a stamp on it, so somebody owes somebody six cents.

Ashore we met some of the officers from H.M.S. *Devonshire*, the large training cruiser that was anchored in the bay. They asked us if we would like to be lifted aboard for a scrub, which seemed a fine idea, so they said that they would see about it.

Their very words: 'Come aboard. Bring your boat.'

Next morning a large naval launch, much larger than us, came over and pulled alongside with a great clanging of bells, to tow us to the cruiser. As we came into the shadow of the huge ship a crane was swung out from somewhere about ten floors up and soon we were swinging through the air in our little boat, looking over the side in horror at the sea sixty feet or more beneath us, only to land gently on her boat deck.

When you say 'We', you mean yourself and Sopranino, *not forgetting Hannibal. I, who had been checking the slings from a whaler, found myself separated from* Sopranino *and home by a long rope ladder and a spindly boat boom, requiring a high order of gymnastics.*

Within half an hour there were three Commanders scrubbing *Sopranino's* bottom at once. Then the Cadets got to work and I counted thirteen paintbrushes in action at the same time. And by nightfall she was painted from stem to stern and from keel to truck.

That night we slept in the Captain's sea cabin, up under the bridge, surrounded by voice-pipes and strange-looking instruments.In the morning *Sopranino* was ready for launching.

Aboard the *Devonshire* we were treated with all naval courtesy, as the Captain's guests. There were moments when this was embarrassing. It is not easy when you come slopping around a corner in your oldest and filthiest overalls, a pot of paint in one hand and a brush in the other, to continue with dignity past an immaculate naval officer and a line of ratings standing stiffly at attention saluting you.

I wanted to go ashore to get some more paint, so I went reverently up to the Officer of the Watch, resplendent in gleaming white and gold on the quarter-deck. Clonk! He came to attention and saluted. Would there be a boat going ashore soon?

'A boat? Certainly, sir.'

He passed the message to another austere figure, who saluted and disappeared through a round hole, like a homing pigeon. Immediately the ship was filled with a dismal wailing: Orders were shouted; men ran around; cranes whirred; and a large twin-engined launch descended from the sky like a spider on its web.

We shot across the bay into the tiny commercial harbour and swept up to the quay with a flourish. I stepped ashore, turning round to ask what time the boat would be going back.

'When you are ready, sir.'

That was one way to go shopping.

But poor Colin got the worst of it. When we were lowered back into the water I cheated, going down on the boat and leaving him to direct operations from above.

Back at the Yacht Club we borrowed an anchor and settled down to a couple of weeks' holiday to celebrate our arrival. Each morning we would drop over the side for a swim in the warm, clear water, then potter around the town or go for a drive in the country with friends. Often we'd come down to the beach around midnight, after a party, to change into our swimming trunks beneath the palm trees in the moonlight, hide our clothes under an upturned boat, and swim back to our home on the water for the night.

Sopranino

Barbados is one of the most beautiful of all the islands of the West Indies, and quite unlike any other. The rest are mountain tops sticking up out of the sea, and look like it, whereas Barbados is a coral island with low hills, fields and fields of sugar cane, palm trees, and great sweeping beaches of glistening white sand pounded out of the coral by the everlasting Atlantic rollers. They run out into the clear green water, with always the cool trade winds to break the heat of the tropical sun.

We got in quite a bit of sailing. We scrounged lifts in the local dinghy classes after racing was finished and often used to sail Sopranino *about the harbour for fun. Sailing inshore is quite different from ocean cruising and was one of the normal things of life that we had found ourselves missing.*

The only real town is Bridgetown, a charming rambling place of winding streets and cool alleys, with women selling piles of native fruit on every corner. The local radio station is a delightful affair. We went in there one day to do a little broadcast, and found the girl announcer reading the news. She had a habit of giggling in the middle of the death notices, so there was a man standing by a big switch to cut her off if she forgot herself.

Her final undoing, I remember, was a commercial about a new stock of men's woollen pants with Balloon Seats.

Then the man came on:

'Today the Weather will be . . . Hey, Pete, what's the weather like?' Pete looked out of the window.

'Fine.'

'The weather will be fine.'

We made our recording and that evening when the announcer said: 'We have here in the studio tonight two . . .' we were standing around the bar discussing with the rest of the boys what those two stupid bastards thought they were up to.

From the town the roads wind outward through the cane fields to the big sugar estates with their processing factories, while along the sheltered coast on the western side lie the houses of those who come down from London and New York for the

142

winter. Just before we left we spent a week-end at one of these, with our little boat anchored off the beach between the reefs. Then off we sailed for Tobago, while our host, Ronald Tree of New York, and David Niven, the film actor, stood on the shore waving us goodbye.

CHAPTER NINE

Windward Islands

Steel Bands—Robinson Crusoe—Where Oysters Grow on Trees—Becalmed in the Gulf of Paria—Mole Crickets and Parasol Ants—Hot Rods and Octopus Racing— One White Man—A Deserted Island—Villa Creek—The Fire Bug—Pigeon Island —Fort de France—Jungle and Dugout Canoes—Hove-to off the Antiguan Coast— Old English Harbour

ONCE more we were out on the ocean sailing, sailing south this time with the easterly trade wind on our beam. A month before, as we arrived at Barbados, we had been delighted by the joy and comfort of this comparatively easy sailing, but now, after a month in harbour with nothing to worry about, it seemed a rough, hard, wet world.

The easiest route from Barbados to the United States would have been to go straight north to Antigua, and this was the route that we had been advised to take, in view of the size of our boat. But having come all those thousands of miles from England we wanted to touch at South America, and at the same time we wanted to make a survey of all the islands of the West Indies for future reference and information.

'*Future reference and information*' *is a wonderful way to be able to describe a cruise in the Caribbean.*

True, the route that we had chosen would be hundreds of miles longer and considerably more difficult, particularly the run up from Trinidad to Grenada, where we should be fighting our way for some sixty miles against the all-powerful trade winds, albeit at an angle. But we were not out to follow the easiest route; we were there to prove that our tiny boat could make any passage that a good sea boat of normal size could undertake in any part of the world.

So off we ran, foaming southward towards Tobago, Robinson Crusoe's island, two hundred miles away. Three days later we were rounding the end of that long thin island, to run down

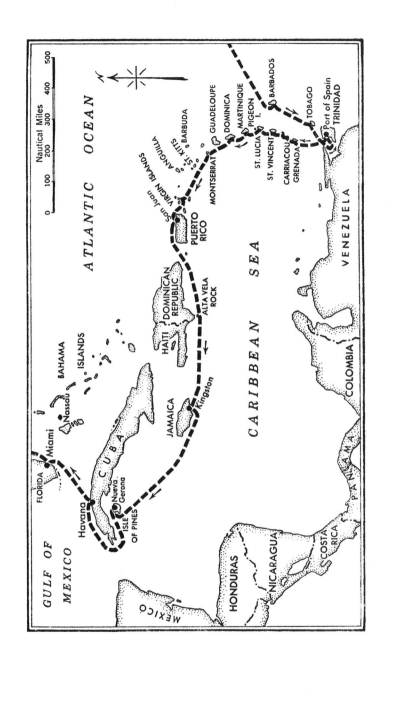

Sopranino

the far side looking for the harbour. We had not been able to get a detailed chart of this place, so all we had to go by was a small smudge on our large chart, marked 'Tobago', and an even smaller dot marked 'Scarborough'. That, then, was the harbour, but just where it was and how one got into it was not clear.

To make matters worse, the easterly trades were blowing almost straight on to the rocky coast, while where we thought the harbour should be was deep in an opening behind a headland. If we were to go too far in and it was not the right one we should have the greatest difficulty in getting out again without being wrecked on one of the outlying rocks.

Still, it looked right and there was nothing else, so in we went, surging forward on the long swells and hoping for the best. Then, as we came nearer, we spotted two beacons on the shore, probably leading marks put there to indicate where the channel lay. We followed them in until, right at the end, close up to the shore, the tiny walled harbour of Scarborough appeared almost beside us.

When we got ashore, the customs officer left his afternoon game of cricket to show us around his island. In a quiet glade we came across a steel-band factory, a palmleaf shack about six feet square where two natives were busy making musical instruments out of old petrol drums. They hammer out a series of patches on the round top of the drum which, when struck, give off different musical notes, depending on their size and shape. Then they saw the barrels off to different heights, according to whether they want a soprano, alto, tenor, or bass instrument.

A steel band consists of a number of each kind of these instruments which, when played together, produce a cheerful brand of music, surprisingly mellow in tone for all its metallic origin.

The great thing about life in all those islands is that the necessities of life are free. If a person has no house he can always sleep under the stars in the cool of the tropical night; the barest rags of clothing suffice to preserve his decency, for it is never cold there; and it has long been a tradition that everyone has a right to eat his fill of the fruit that grows in such abundance.

In those conditions people have time for music and laughter and song and everywhere you go you will find them singing. Even carpenters working on a building will be singing, keeping time to their music with the beats of their hammers.

That evening we spent listening to one of the steel bands, out of doors under the trees with the tropical moonlight filtering down through their branches. The next morning we sailed around to the southern tip of the island, where we were piloted into our first real lagoon to have lunch on the beach under the waving palms and pick oysters off the trees.

You really can pick oysters off the trees. There is a tide of a few feet, and at high tide the oysters cling to the roots of the mangroves, so that at low tide you can walk along the beach plucking them off, fresh and eatable.

From there to the Bocas del Dragon, the Dragon's Teeth which guard the entrance to Port of Spain, Trinidad, is only about seventy miles and barely took us a day to cover. But there we found that the ocean current constantly sweeps out through the four narrow passes between the high cliffs. We tried each one in turn with the same result, until in the end we had to sail right over to the Venezuelan coast and far down the Gulf of Paria, almost to the mouth of the Orinoco River, before we could swing round and let the current sweep us back up to the harbour.

All across the Gulf of Paria the water is dark-green from the outflow of the Orinoco. It was in these waters that we had been warned to look out for the giant sea snakes, the anacondas, that could swallow a man whole. In fact we never saw one and really we were not sorry, but it gave us something to think about, alone on watch in the darkness, as we drifted round the Gulf.

The water there was a fine, thick, treacly green in which it was a pleasure to wash our red plastic spoons.

Each time we put our nose into one of these passes we would lose our wind, to be swept out again by the current.

Sopranino

At last the harbour of Port of Spain came into view. Houses clustered up on the hills overlooking the gulf, as we passed close along the shores of Trinidad Island and scared a cloud of pelicans off the wreck of an old-time sailing ship that lay half sunken in the mud. It had taken us fifty-one hours of drifting and sailing to cover those last ten miles.

Port of Spain is a cosmopolitan town, full of people of all races and creeds. We were fascinated by the beautiful Chinese and half-Chinese girls on the streets and the colourful array of Chinese, East Indians, West Indians, and Europeans who came riding in on surf-boards to land on beautiful Maraccas beach at the week-ends.

The famous asphalt lake is unimpressive to look at, something like an abandoned airfield, though the stuff goes down solid for Lord knows how far, bubbling up from the depths as fast as it is taken away.

While we were at Port of Spain we were moored at the pier belonging to the harbour pilots, and one day they took us out in an outgoing ship, introducing us to the Captain as apprentice pilots learning the trade.

Standing on the bridge of that great ship, which seemed to tower over the town and was pointing straight at it, we were horrified to hear the pilot calmly give the order: 'Full ahead'.

We had visions of fetching up in the market place, but he knew his business all right and she swung around in a great arc, passing neatly out of the entrance. We followed him down the long ladder slung over the steel side of the ship, to leap on to the pilot launch, bobbing alongside.

The northern tip of Venezuela, on the continent of South America, runs out in a long point to within about fifteen miles of Trinidad (which is really a detached part of that continent) with the result that there are dangerous snakes, particularly the mortal fer-de-lance, in the jungle that comes right up to the suburban houses.

Our host at dinner one evening told us he had had quite a time in his own back yard, fighting a five-foot fer-de-lance in the dark, a broomstick in one hand and a torch in the other.

Windward Islands

To make things more exciting the torch kept going on and off, to the dismay of man and snake alike. However, he won and all was well. They take their wild life as it comes down there.

As a matter of fact it is a good thing that they do, for they really have some of the cussedest creatures around. As soon as the English arrive out there they promptly plant a garden. Then, as the flowers come up, the fun starts. A man will go out one morning to find his precious flowers slowly descending into the earth. It will be a mole cricket at work. They burrow under the surface, saw off the plants at the roots, and pull them down into the ground.

Then, when he is having supper in his house, with a nice bowl of flowers on the table beside him, the Parasol Ants will come in—thousands of them—climbing up the legs of the table to nip off a leaf or a part of a leaf each, sling it over their shoulders, swarm down to the floor, and disappear out of the window with it. It is impossible to stop them. If you clap your hands or make a loud noise the long line of leaves across the floor will stop for a moment, to move on again a few seconds later, until in half an hour there will be nothing left of the flowers but a bunch of bare stalks.

We had heard that we would have to have a special permit before we could land in Venezuela, so we went along to see the consul of that country. He was most charming but regretted that he had no power to issue such a permit. It would be possible to obtain one, yes, but it would take some weeks for the formalities to be got through.

We were very disappointed and a little sad that after overcoming all the hazards of the sea for nearly five thousand miles we should be prevented from setting foot in South America by a purely artificial barrier, but there it was. We still had well over three thousand miles of water to cover before our task would be completed and we had neither the time nor the money to wait weeks for a permit.

Already we had been within spitting distance of Venezuela as we came in around the Gulf of Paria, so we let it go at that.

Sopranino

As far as we were concerned we had been to South America.

Now we had reached the most southerly part of our voyaging, and for the next thousand miles we would be going northward, following the chain of the Windward and the Leeward islands towards Antigua. We had completed two sections of the voyage, the passage down to Africa and the crossing of the ocean, but we still had a great deal ahead of us.

There was the difficult beat up to Grenada for a start, and after that the long haul up the chain of islands to Antigua. Then there would be the run down past the Virgin Islands, Puerto Rico, the Dominican Republic, and Haiti, to Jamaica and around the end of Cuba to Miami. And even there we would not be finished, for we would still have more than a thousand miles of the American coastline to cover before we reached New York.

And at any time, at any minute in any hour in all those weeks and months ahead, one small mistake could put us on the rocks and the expedition would be finished. Every moment that we were at sea we would have to be on our guard, while in port there would be work to be done—cleaning, painting, and repairing to keep the ship in shape—rules and regulations to be understood and overcome and a constant watch to be kept for thieves who might steal some valuable and irreplaceable piece of equipment.

Life really is much more difficult cruising inshore, and so very much more hazardous, other things being even.

Personally, I never allowed myself to think of reaching New York. The task seemed too remote and complicated. So I would set myself a seemingly possible goal to achieve and work towards that, and for the moment it was to reach Antigua.

So we schemed and planned, discussing with friends we met the best ways of dealing with everything from whip sharks and sting rays to the overpowering heat of the sun that by now was almost overhead at midday and would remain so as we went north, knowing all the time that at each little stage we would have to re-scheme and re-plan to meet the conditions as they changed.

Windward Islands

As we had hoped and believed, our little ship took the beat up to Grenada better than the experts had predicted and soon that island, the first of the long chain of mountain tops, rose out of the sea ahead of us in a great volcanic cone some thirty miles across.

Like most of these islands it has one main harbour, St George's, on the sheltered western side. The town itself is built on a series of steep little hills clustered round the harbour, so that when you tie up to the quayside you face a row of shops with street after street rising up behind it. The roads are so steep and narrow that when driving you have to stop fifty yards before each crossroads, to wait until the policeman on duty waves you on.

Leander, the large yacht to which we had tied up when first we had arrived in Barbados, was there as we sailed in. After due celebration we went out around the steep, winding mountain roads with the local Hot-Rod Club, streaking along the edges of precipices as our drivers pointed down into the steaming jungle far below, remarking casually:

'Old Charlie went over there last week. He misjudged his turn.'

As far as I could gather, the whole idea for the sports car club came from the number of saloons that had had their tops bashed in through falling into gorges, thus becoming open cars. The boys took us one day to a beach at the top end of the island, and there we had a swim and a picnic. Rum punch out of an icebox in the trunk of the car and coconuts from the nearest tree.

Then down on to the reef to look for, of all things, octopuses. When they were found they were taken in hand and, when a suitable field had been assembled, the day's racing would start. The octopuses were fortunately quite small and travelled when flat out at a quick walking pace. Each pussy jet-propelled himself across the lagoon with his jockey following close behind. I observed from a cautious distance.

Soon we had completed our jobs for that harbour and were ready to leave. An attractive young English girl was holding our line. Hesitating, she turned to her older companion:

'Shall I let them go?'

Sopranino

'You'll have to pull yourself together and do it sometime.'

'Beast.'

And off we sailed towards remote Cariacou, to arrive there in the middle of the night, creeping up in the dark between the hidden reefs and looking for the flickering oil lamp that serves as the only beacon, to anchor off the jetty.

In the morning we awoke to find ourselves swinging nicely between several local trading sloops, none of which had had lights on them the night before. The little jetty was crowded with people unloading the sloops one at a time as they came alongside and piling in vast numbers into an incredibly top-heavy motorboat that ran the only passenger service to Grenada.

Behind, a line of shacks and huts showed through the palms along the shore, with one small stone building, at the head of the jetty, that served as customs house, police station, jail, and administrative offices. Various odd-looking native craft came over to visit us.

After a while a dignified dark gentleman came over in a small boat to inquire in a puzzled voice whether there was a yacht coming up from Grenada. We told him that we were it and he looked even more puzzled. It seemed that he was the district officer in charge of the island, and he had received a radio message in code from the governor in Grenada saying that a yacht that had crossed the Atlantic Ocean from England would be calling at his island.

He had come out, looking for some large and luxurious vessel, and all he could find was little *Sopranino* bouncing on the waves off the end of his jetty. However, once he got over the shock he was most helpful, taking us to see the old fort and introducing us to the one white man on the island, a Catholic priest.

He took a subtle revenge for his surprise by inviting us to be guests at a Girl Guides' concert.

Everywhere you go through the islands you find forts, more often than not with their brass cannon still in place. Most of the islands changed hands between the Spanish and the French and the English several times, not so long ago, and each time

152

the fort would be destroyed and a new one built on top of it. So now they look like layer cakes, with strata of different kinds of architecture to show how often they have changed hands.

It is interesting to note that Barbados alone stayed out of that struggle, remaining British all the time for the simple reason that the sailing warships of that time could not make the hundred-odd miles out to windward against the trade winds to get there, whereas they could charge happily up and down the line of the others as often as they pleased.

In fact, Barbados even remained aloof from the Civil War in England. There is an old law there that is still in force that if any man shall call another a Cavalier or a Roundhead he shall be forced to buy him, together with all witnesses present, a turkey dinner.

A farewell drink in the only hotel, where you sit by lamplight as Mine Host takes the bottle of rum from the dresser and puts it on the bare table in front of you, and we set off up the Grenadines, a chain of tiny islands, mostly uninhabited, that lies between Cariacou and the next large island, St Vincent.

Not far from Cariacou there is a group of three of these islets, called the Tobago Cays, alone out in the ocean in a lagoon surrounded by reefs. We sailed in between the Cays to anchor for the night, swimming ashore with knives in our teeth, in case of sharks, to explore our first uninhabited island.

We made our way separately up the rocky slope through the thick green vegetation to the top, from where we could see our little boat swinging peacefully to her anchor in the lagoon below. Coming down, I was picking my way carefully step by step over the rocks and crevices through the bush when there was a loud *Plop!* and I found myself face to face with a giant iguana, a species of lizard perhaps four feet long, looking more like a medieval dragon than anything else, and very large on the rock above me.

I don't think that they are really dangerous, but I never stopped to go into the matter. With a slither and a bump I hit that beach in no seconds flat and swam back to the ship to have supper as the sun went down.

153

Sopranino

It is strange, but there was far more sense of loneliness there among those wild little islands than ever there was when we were many hundreds of miles from land on the wide Atlantic Ocean. Out there you did not expect to find people, but with land around you with no people on it you felt a sense of desolation, so that I for one was quite glad to sail on to the northward once more.

Reaching up the Grenadines, counting off each rock or islet on our chart as we passed it, we sailed by Becque with its little township looking for all the world like any small Breton village. We finally drifted into Villa Creek, St Vincent, that lies between the main island and a small wooded islet with green lawns and white houses showing between the trees that come down to the water's edge.

Next to the wooden jetty where we were moored was the island's air base—one large shed marked 'customs' and a ramp down into the water, at the top of which sat a six-seater flying boat that buzzed industriously off every few hours, taking passengers to the other islands.

The regular pilot went down with influenza, which is very easy to catch in the Tropics, and a fresh one was flown up from Trinidad in a small private plane. He made an error in his approach to the grass field beside the creek, spinning into the ground from three hundred feet. The aircraft was a total wreck but the two men miraculously escaped, and next morning as we left for St Lucia the flying boat roared low overhead, the pilot swathed in bandages, on its scheduled flight.

Like all the mountain-top islands, St Vincent is high. So high that there is no wind at all on the safe western side near the shore and you have to drift out as much as five miles to find a breeze to take you to the next island, following the route of the native sloops and schooners that carry most of the goods from island to island.

Then, for a brief twenty miles or so, we came into the full force of the trade wind as we rode over the ocean swells that surge between the islands, to run up under the shelter of St Lucia into Castries Harbour at its northern end.

Windward Islands

The town of Castries has a firebug. Every year they build the town up and every year he burns it down again. One of these days they are going to get cross with him. It also has thieves, so we moved over to a quiet deserted creek nearby to careen our ship in the traditional manner of the islands and scrub her bottom.

There is very little rise and fall of tide round that part of the world, so that one cannot set a ship up on the shore and wait for the water level to fall to scrub the weed off the bottom. But it is vital that any boat shall have her bottom cleaned frequently in those waters, or the dreaded teredo worm will find its way through a gap in the protective coating.

Though no larger than a pin when it enters, one worm can grow rapidly inside the wood planking of a boat to a length of several feet, eating its way through the planks and timbers and leaving behind it a hole as thick as a man's finger.

They never come out of the wood again, so there is no sign of their existence except a small pinhole near the water line, until suddenly one day the whole ship falls apart. So every six weeks we had to clean *Sopranino's* bottom thoroughly and examine it closely for the telltale pinholes.

In every small commercial harbour in the West Indies you will find careening docks, where the local sloops and schooners go to be careened. Ropes are taken from the masts to the quayside and tightened down until the ship is lying almost on her side in the water with her masts over the roadway. Then men go around in boats to scrub and paint the exposed bottom, turning her round later to repeat the process on the other side.

But for our little ship the stone jetty in the creek was sufficient. Standing on it, we could pull our mast down by hand and tie it there while we worked in the sunshine, as native canoes, made from hollowed-out logs, went sailing by laden down with produce for the market.

When we had finished our work we decided to take an afternoon off. Just off the northwest corner of St Lucia there lies a small island, perhaps a mile long by half-a-mile wide, that is probably the most beautiful in all the Caribbean. It is called

Sopranino

Pigeon Island and is leased by the government to a Mrs Lee, a member of the old D'Oyly Carte Opera Company, who runs it as a sort of guest house for visiting yachtsmen. Money won't buy you a place there. If she doesn't like you or you misbehave, out you go. But if she likes you, you are welcome to her palm-thatched bar where you can sit looking out through the trees across the clear lagoon, with no sound but the lapping of the waves and the rattle of the palms as they sway in the breeze, exchanging news and tales of other ocean voyagers that have passed that way and now are dead or in distant lands.

Behind the bar you walk up steep grassy paths, past three or four small, round native huts that she keeps for her guests, to the old look-out post high on the top of the hill where Admiral Rodney used to stand looking over towards where the French fleet lay in Martinique, thirty miles away.

But we had no time to remain in that enchanted isle and as darkness fell we slipped our lines, to drift out of the lagoon and lay our course for Martinique, rising and dipping over the swell as the island faded into the darkness behind us and was gone.

Fort-de-France, the capital of Martinique, is a typical French provincial town. By our standards the streets are dirty, the plumbing is primeval, and the food is magnificent. But always we must go on, on to the northward.

Dominica, the next island, has its principal town, Roseau, in the south. We called there to clear customs, but found it a dreary place. The cruise ships had taken to calling there and now it had an atmosphere of spivs out to fleece the visitor, so we left within the hour for Portsmouth, at the northern end of the island. Sailing up the coast in the dark, we noticed a native schooner bearing down upon us with no lights. We changed course. She did the same, always closing in on us in the moonlight.

At that point we were very far from any sort of civilisation, alone on the water off a virtually uninhabited section of wild mountainous coastline. We had heard many stories of boats disappearing mysteriously in those parts and knew that even today the local boys are not above a bit of piracy on the high seas.

A few years earlier a friend of mine had been sailing in a similar bleak spot off the Malayan coast and had run into a gang of pirates. They found his body some weeks later on the beach. He had been killed for his watch and his small change.

So we doused our lights and made two or three quick changes of course, creeping in under the dark coastline where, unlit, we would be very hard to follow. We brought out our automatic pistol and placed it on deck, together with our Very flare-pistol (a murderous weapon at short range), and sat quietly waiting for the fun to start.

But she slid by about half a mile to seaward of us, creaking in the darkness, and after giving her time to get well clear ahead we went on our way, to sail into deep mountain-encircled Portsmouth Bay just before dawn.

It is almost unbelievable that such a wonderful remote, wild spot should exist in the world today. No ships call there and there are no telephones, radios, or even roads connecting it with the outside world. There is a track, traversable by a jeep, that winds over the mountains part of the way down the centre of the island and then peters out. There is a similar track running up from Roseau towards the north, but they have never been joined because the people in the north do not like the people in the south and the people in the south think nothing of the people in the north, and neither of them see any reason for communicating with the other.

As we sat having breakfast, lying to our anchor off the native village, the Big White Chief came over in his launch to greet us and invite us over to his estate in the evening. Later he came back in his jeep, down to the shore, to fetch us. We waved hopefully, signalling that we wanted to be taken ashore. He clapped his hands and shouted something, and immediately a whole fleet of native dugout canoes converged on us. We each balanced ourselves precariously in one of these strange craft as the oarsmen paddled furiously and we skimmed over the water to the beach.

Sopranino

There are four or five white men on that end of the island, principally engaged in growing limes. When they want a house, they just clear a space in the jungle and start building, and if they want to go anywhere they bump along the beach in a jeep. The roads are practically non-existent and the jungle is unusually solid and thick.

We were told about the doctor who went along the beach for ten miles, then inland up the course of a stream for five, and decided to walk home through the jungle. It took him fourteen days to cover the twelve-odd miles.

But we had to press on. We heard that Guadeloupe, the next island, was similar to Martinique, being also French, and it hardly seemed worth our while to go through all the formalities of the customs to visit it, so we stood well out to sea and sailed on past it towards Antigua.

That island is almost circular in shape, with its port and principal town of St Johns on the far side. But on the bleak, almost deserted side nearest us lay Admiral Nelson's Old English Harbour, where only a couple of hundred years ago the British Fleet used to sail in for repairs after their battles with the French, and it was there that we had decided to go.

And one bright dawn, there it lay across the deep-blue sea ahead of us, brown tinged with green, rocky and rugged, with the white breakers exploding along its shores.

The great thing about Old English Harbour, from the naval point of view, is that it is almost impossible to find unless you know just where it is. Time and time again the French Fleet had sailed up and down that bleak coast, looking for the entrance, without ever finding it.

We had detailed instructions and a chart to show us exactly where it was, but still we could not see it. Each rocky little bay looked exactly like the next, and none of them showed the least sign of leading anywhere.

We closed the coast to examine it more thoroughly, and were sailing along, not far from the rocks, when down came one of the sudden tropical squalls, blotting out all visibility in the driving rain and whipping up the seas into a froth.

Windward Islands

We clawed a little way off the shore and hove to until it had passed over, then back again to continue our search. We nosed our way cautiously between the rocks into the deep, narrow little bay where it should be. There was no sign of anything. Suddenly we spotted the old fortress and in a moment the entrance opened up almost behind us.

Inside, we sailed across the calm water towards the still, silent docks. This was it. Antigua. Almost a thousand miles from Barbados, with all the Windward and the Leeward islands behind us. One more task was completed.

As we drifted alongside the low quay Commander Nicholson, who lives alone in the old dockyard with his wife, came out to hail us: 'Hallo. We were expecting you.'

They run a charter service among the islands with two yachts, one captained by each of their two sons, and one of them had spotted us coming and radioed them.

The dockyard, with its careening capstans, spar lofts, barracks, workshops, and Nelson's house, is just as the Admiral left it. Looking round the silent buildings you can almost see the shipwrights and seamen busy repairing and refitting their battle-scarred wooden ships, while the soldiers in their red coats march to and fro, drilling on the parade ground.

But now all is quiet and peaceful there, making it an ideal place to spend a week cleaning and painting our little ship before tackling the next run, westward to Cuba.

Those were good days, relaxing in a safe harbour after the weeks of the worry and strain of working our ship northward over strange seas, in and out of countless strange harbours. Each day we worked on the boat, cleaning and checking, preparing for the thousands of miles ahead, and in the cool of the evening we would dive into the still dark waters for a swim, watching the turtles feeding off the weed on the stone walls of the dock, and go over to the Nicholsons' to swap tales of far-away places.

Soon *Sopranino* was ready again, and then, just as we were about to leave, a radio message came through. One of Commander Nicholson's sons had just been taken ill on

Guadeloupe. The other had come in a couple of days before in the fine large 104-foot ketch *Maria Katherina*, so they invited us to go with them in her to Guadeloupe.

It was strange for us to be aboard that big yacht, with her wide decks, her towering masts, and her heavy substantial gear, ploughing through the seas at a steady six knots to the southward.

I for one was quite scared to be on such a large ship and worried about what one would do if something were to go wrong away up there at the top of those enormous masts. On the other hand, what could anyone wish more than hot Bovril served in the lee of the deckhouse at eleven o'clock exactly, with the heat of the sun and the cool of the breeze?

I remember the next morning, alone at the wheel in the early light as we came back to Antigua, thinking of all that vast weight heaving and straining over the seas and of how much happier and safer I should feel in our own tiny vessel.

And within a few hours we were away in her once again, bound for the Virgin Islands.

CHAPTER TEN

Westward to Cuba

Past St Martin and Sabre—Round Rock Passage—Our First Contact with America—
Dreaming of Beer—We Are Held up at Knife-point—Colin Doubles for Arlene Dahl
—Our Last Run Together—Caught by a Tropical Storm off the Reefs—Nueva
Gerona, Isle of Pines—Colin Flies for Home—Patrick Carries on Alone

WITH our wind free we fairly raced up past St Martin and the strange little Dutch island of Sabre, round and high, shaped just like a battered bowler hat, that has a town called Top at the bottom and a town called Bottom at the top.

On our way we met the famous cruising yacht, *Tern III*, beating her way south towards Antigua. She had taken five days to get there from Tortola, in the Virgin Islands, while we, with the wind behind us, made the same journey in the other direction in two.

Three of the Virgins—St Thomas, Tortola, and Gorda—lie close together, and outside them there stretches a long chain of rocks, two or three miles offshore. Some of them are large and obvious, while others lie under the water, out of sight but highly dangerous.

There are a couple of safe passages between them, but the problem is to find one. Each rock looks the same as the next. Once again we had not been able to get detailed charts of the entrance, so up and down we sailed, checking landmarks and trying to identify the various groups from written notes that we had been given in Antigua.

Finally we found what we were pretty sure was Round Rock Passage, though Round Rock was anything but round from where we were. Anyway we decided to try it and ran in, holding our breath for a moment as we passed between the rocks, waiting for the bump. But it never came. We had guessed right, and now we were inside, sailing across the wide sound towards Tortola, to drift into the narrow lonely bay just after dark, on the last of the dying breeze.

Soon it died altogether, leaving us drifting, becalmed, on the dark mirror of the water. I was below cooking up a little something hot when suddenly Colin called:

'Patrick.'

'Yes?'

'We're drifting backwards. What's behind us?'

I glanced at the chart:

'Rocks.'

'Better sling out an anchor.'

'Good idea.' I turned out the stove and went on deck. Over went the anchor and out went the line, to stop with a jerk, straight up and down.

'No bottom', I muttered. 'We'll have to row.'

Out came the paddle, but we couldn't find the rowlock anywhere. Hurriedly I looked in all the likely and unlikely places, while the current swept us back and back towards the rocks at the entrance.

I never did find it that night, but as I was on my knees, turning out the locker, with a great pile of stuff around me, he called down again:

'Don't look now, but I think I've found a breeze.'

I went on deck. A tiny breath of air from astern was easing us forward over the water, just beating the current. For two hours we juggled with our sails, adjusting them to catch each puff, sometimes gaining a little, sometimes slipping back, until at last we reached the shallow water by the jetty where we could anchor for the rest of the night.

Tortola is one of the British Virgin Islands, a wild, lonely place of high mountains and narrow valleys. Nothing much happens there: a little farming, a little fishing, and that is about all.

It has one claim to fame; it is only a few miles from the American island of St Thomas and its life is so closely linked with that island that for convenience they use dollars as the standard currency. It must have been about the only place in the world that had at that time a free and legal exchange between the pound and the dollar.

Patrick went into the local store to buy himself a packet of cigarettes. First he asked how much they would be and was a little surprised to find them rather more expensive than elsewhere, but of course there are shipping charges and customs duty. Then the storeman handed him a packet of not twenty but two hundred cigarettes.

Unfortunately we only had a few pounds with us, but what we had we changed into dollars, before sailing on around to Charlotte Amalie, on St Thomas.

If you arrive after hours in St Thomas, you have to pay overtime for the Customs man and the Immigration man and the Health man and the Mayor and the Privy Council. We hoisted every sail in the ship to try and get there in time. Though normally the most we can carry at one time is three sails, we found weird and wonderful ways of hanging up five altogether and even pressed our big ensign into service as an extra, but still we arrived a quarter of an hour late.

What a difference! St Thomas, that had been bought by America from the Danes, was a thriving resort, specialising in honeymoons and divorces. It was our first contact with the United States and, though it would be many weeks before we would reach America, still here we could hoist our American courtesy flag for the first time.

As it went up, to flutter in the breeze from the starboard spreader, I remembered the day when we had bought it, back in far-off England, over eight months before. Then our destination had been a carefully kept secret and we had wrapped it inside a bundle of other things in case anyone saw it as we took it aboard.

Now it flew proudly over our little ship, paying our respects to the port. And, who knew?—a couple of thousand miles more and it might be flying in America itself. But for the moment we were content to go ashore to a drugstore and have a Coca-Cola by way of celebration.

A couple of days later Colin came back aboard, about eight in the morning, looking a little pale, and said in a firm voice:

'We sail within the hour.'

Sopranino

Long ago, at the start of the trip, it had been agreed that if either of us ever said that, we sailed within the hour and no silly questions asked. So up went those sails and out of that harbour we went. Outside he said:

'Where are we going to?'

'San Juan. Puerto Rico.'

'How far is that?'

'About sixty miles.'

He looked thoughtful: 'Do they have aeroplanes there?'

'I expect so, but you'll be all right. . . . What was she like?'

'Shut up.'

I shut up.

I smell a calumny. My recollection of our departure from Charlotte Amalie begins with our meeting at the boat one morning. We went on board together and without a word cast off and hoisted sails and away. It might be that I did mutter the magic words, but if so I only got them in first by a short head.

We cut through the straits between St Thomas and Puerto Rico, to go bowling down the north coast of that island before the wind. From far away we could see the spires and domes of the city of San Juan glittering in the sunlight and as we closed in to the shore we could make out the fortress on the hill that stands guard over the entrance to the harbour.

As we approached, a destroyer of the U.S. Navy came up from behind us. I was sitting as usual, on watch, in bathing trunks and the large girl's straw hat, quietly smoking my pipe, when there were loud wolf-whistles from behind. I think it must have given them rather a shock when I turned around, for they sheered off and disappeared into the harbour.

The town of San Juan lies on a long neck of land, with the harbour between it and the mainland. As you go up the river the docks thin out and give way to private houses until, right at the end by the bridge, you come to the magnificent Yacht Club, a four-story block built over the water, with docks for boats underneath it and luxurious bars and lounges above.

Although Puerto Rico is American it shows a strong Spanish influence and much more Spanish than English is spoken. It is very glamorous and very expensive and at that time we were not very well off, having spent nine of our eleven dollars in St Thomas, so we paid our harbour dues, bought a loaf of bread, and prepared to leave.

As we were standing on the club steps a fellow Englishman came down to see us. He was working on a motor fishing vessel, running down two thousand miles through the Panama Canal to fish off the Galapagos Islands in the Pacific Ocean and then coming back two thousand miles to Puerto Rico to sell the catch. But apparently it paid. Strange are the ways of commerce.

Just as he was letting go our lines a local yachtsman came down with a large anchor. He said that he had got it for his boat and then sold the boat, so that now he had an anchor and no boat. Would we like it? We certainly would. For the last thousand miles through the islands we had been making do with a heavy and not very effective thing that we had traded for our two winches, back in Trinidad. But now we had a real anchor again, a very comforting thought.

We were keen to get on, particularly as Colin had to be in Bermuda by the beginning of July and it was already the middle of May, so we decided to miss Haiti and carry straight on with the 650-odd miles to Jamaica.

That was a good run. With the wind nearly behind us we swept down through the wide channel between Puerto Rico and Haiti, across the 100-mile sweep of the coast of that large island to round the Alta Vela rock and lay our course for Kingston.

The channel between Puerto Rico and Haiti is the famous Mona Passage, where the buccaneers came from.

Sometimes, off those coasts, there would be showers. They did not last long, but while they did they came down so hard they beat the water flat, while the raindrops that hit the boat bounced up a foot off the deck. In a way we welcomed them, for it was very hot and they gave us a chance of a shower in fresh water.

We had given up swimming for the time being, as we were coming into the waters where the barracuda abound. The

165

Sopranino

natives call them 'cross fish' and they really are a vicious lot.
If a shark makes a pass at you, you can usually reckon to scare
him off by splashing or making a loud noise, but a barracuda
will come right on in and get his dinner.

We had heard that in some areas they are quite harmless, but
just where those areas lay was open to some doubt. Anyway,
we weren't taking any chances. We did have some packets of
shark-repellent that we had got in England before we left, in
case we had a job to do under water at sea, though we had no
information on its efficiency against barracudas.

It had been concocted for me by a chemist friend and it made
a dark stain on the water, the same as that made by an octopus,
of which sharks are scared. When he gave it to me he said:

'By the way, you'd better be careful. It may attract the
octopuses.'

I had vision of bringing vast numbers of those horrible
creatures swarming up from the depths of the ocean, hellbent
for a party, and put the packets away far at the bottom of the
deepest locker for emergency use only.

We did see one whale on that run, though. Our only one
on the whole trip and totally unexpected in those latitudes. He
was a couple of hundred yards from us, vastly bigger than we
were, banging his tail furiously on the water. One blow from
that tail would have crushed our little craft like an eggshell.
We sat watching him rather anxiously for a while. There must
have been a good ten feet of that shiny black tail rearing straight
up in the air, with a great flat fin on the end of it. It would
pause for a moment, then down it would come to hit the water
with a resounding crash, sending up a plume of spray like a
small depth-charge.

We decided that either he was having trouble with some
other monstrous sea creature or merely knocking the barnacles
off himself, but as we drew away from him the noise stopped
and he disappeared, so we never really knew the answer.

*A short while later a large marlin shot past us at high speed, standing
vertically on the water and skidding along on his tail, eyeing us balefully
as he passed.*

Westward to Cuba

The next day our log line stopped going round for the first time. We pulled it in to find that it had been neatly bitten off three or four feet from the heavy brass spinner at the end. Whatever it was had presumably swallowed the spinner and also the lead weight ahead of it. We hoped it gave him indigestion.

Probably it was just a shark. We had been told that they were particularly numerous thereabouts and had a habit of swallowing log spinners, so there was no point in putting out our second one. We might as well keep that for use later on in more civilised places; meanwhile we should have to do without it and estimate our distances run from hour to hour.

Soon we were running in towards Jamaica, straining ahead into the darkness to catch a glimpse of Morant Point lighthouse, full of enthusiasm and thoughts of cold beer. As I sat below in the cabin cooking supper I could hear Colin singing something to the tune of 'The St Louis Blues'. I listened for a moment to the words coming clearly down above the roar of the stove:

'I hate to feel . . . that evening Stew go down.'

Ingrate. I'd fix him. I'd fry him a sausage. Let him try and keep that on his plate, with the ship rolling the way she was.

Just after midnight we saw the loom of a light, glowing in the sky ahead of us, and quite soon the lighthouse was flashing away, beckoning us on towards Jamaica. In the morning the island was high and green beside us as we ran down the coast, looking for the entrance to Kingston Harbour.

That is a particularly nasty entrance for a major port. You have to make a long run in, close to the shore, with the seas breaking on outlying rocks and islands all around you. But we were lucky this time. We had managed to get a chart of the entrance in Puerto Rico, so in we went, checking off the buoys and markers as we passed each one and following the narrow twisting channel as it swung around into the shelter of the land.

As you go in through the narrow entrance, Kingston itself lies on the far side of a huge natural harbour, perhaps a mile wide by several miles long. And such is the shape of the surrounding mountains that every day the wind sweeps across it at full gale force, whipping up quite a sea for a small boat.

Sopranino

Obviously there would be no point in anchoring out in that, so we ran in to the derelict-looking quay at old Port Royal, a couple of miles away from the town across the wide harbour and some fifteen if you go round by road.

As we made fast to the old jetty, still avidly dreaming of beer but never daring to hope to get outside any for some time yet, a tall lanky figure appeared, looking down on us from the top of a pile of rubble.

'Hi, fellas. My name's Tony. Come and have a beer.'

It was Sir Anthony Jenkinson, who was setting up a boat-yard there, and he really did have beer. Cold beer. Long may his name be remembered.

That afternoon, as we sat in the shade outside his office, we washed our beers down with thirty-two Coca-Colas between us. We really must have been thirsty. He confirmed what we had read about the gales that blow every day across the harbour and advised us to remain at his dock, commuting into town whenever necessary on the local ferry boat.

He also told us that there had been a minor hurricane in Antigua that had caused quite a lot of trouble. We worked out the dates. We must just have missed it and been in Tortola when it struck, though up there, two hundred miles from Antigua, we had not felt it at all.

Jamaica itself had had a really bad hurricane two years previously that had curled round the mountains to blow in gusts of 140 miles an hour from all different directions, causing widespread destruction.

Big ships had been unable to remain in position, even with all their anchors out and their powerful engines running full ahead against the storm, and had been driven helplessly across the harbour. Some of them had collided and sunk, while others had been driven high up on the shore.

Ashore, solidly built brick houses that had withstood storms for hundreds of years fell like packs of cards, killing those inside. Port Royal, in particular, looked as if it had been hit by an air raid, with piles of rubble and wreckage strewn all over the place.

Westward to Cuba

Already it was nearly the end of May and the hurricane season was due to start at any time. We should have to keep an eye on the weather from now on.

We were now nearly a thousand miles from Antigua and it was time we put some more work in on the boat, so we stayed in Port Royal for two weeks, cleaning, checking, and painting. We went over by ferry to the Yacht Club to collect and answer vast quantities of mail that had been waiting for us there.

Mail is one of the big problems on a trip of this nature. It takes so long for letters to go to and from Europe, particularly from some of the smaller islands, that by the time the answers come back, if they do ever catch up with you, they no longer make sense. And trying to organise anything, such as the delivery of a spare part, without actually sitting for months in one place waiting for it, is an almost impossible task.

Coming back one night from the Club, about midnight, we were walking alone and unarmed through the deserted streets down towards the docks, discussing something and not paying a great deal of attention to the shadows in the doorways as we strolled through the long dark colonnades past rows of empty shops.

Suddenly we noticed an evil-looking dark character following us, quietly catching us up. I had a feeling that all was not on the level, so we crossed over to the other side of the street where the open pavement was flanked by railings with empty buildings behind them.

The character crossed over behind us. At the same time two more who had been hiding in the shadows further up the colonnade came padding across in front of us. In a moment they were around us in a semicircle, the ugly-looking knives in their hands flashing in the moonlight.

I glanced down at the knives. They were held downwards, with the thumb on the blade. These boys knew how to use them. You can take a gun off a man if there is only one of him, but a knife properly used at close quarters is a different matter, and three knives are quite a proposition.

Our job in life was to get that boat safely to the United States and starting a row with the local mobsters at that stage would only land us in hospital and might set us back weeks. We had better play this one with a little skill.

Colin had a miniature camera in his hand and I had a fair amount of money on me, neither of which we could afford to lose. The leader was the first one we had seen and he was up my end. I tried to look casual and said:

'Sorry, boys, you're out of luck. We've been out for the evening and spent all our money. That's all we've got left between us.'

I took my hand out of my pocket with a handkerchief, some small change, and one Jamaican pound in it, and held it out for him to see.

Obviously we had done the right thing to move over into the open, for they were all three very nervous—more so, probably, than we were—and obviously keen to get away as soon as possible. On the other hand, the leader had to get something or his prestige with his boys would be ruined.

He took the pound I offered him, muttered something, and they slid away down a side street into the darkness. They had got seven shillings each out of the deal and we had had an interesting experience and collected a nice little story to bore our friends with in our old age, so one way and another everybody was satisfied with the evening's entertainment.

Next morning we reported the matter to the police and asked for a permit to bring a gun ashore in future. They told us we were lucky to get away with it as there had been quite a number of people stabbed recently, and promptly gave us the gun licence.

I asked the officer what the form was on firing the thing, if similar circumstances should arise again.

'Shoot to kill before they strike', he remarked casually, without looking up from the papers on his desk.

Back at the dock we inquired from the customs officer what papers we should require for our arrival in the United States. Among the many was a Deratisation Certificate, to certify that we had no rats aboard. We went back and peered into little

Westward to Cuba

Sopranino, wondering how on earth any rat could find room to squeeze aboard. And sure enough, in the after locker, there were four of them, brand new-ones barely a few days old. The mother was nowhere to be seen, but we had to take every single thing ashore and disinfect the boat throughout before we could get our certificate.

We had just finished putting it all back and were almost ready to leave when Sir Anthony Jenkinson remarked that he was taking his native-built schooner round to the north coast of the island to make some location shots for a new Technicolor movie that Paramount were making. He needed a couple of crew for the job. Would we like to earn a few pounds?

We never turned down a chance of earning a little money, so we shut the lid on our boat and sailed off with him for Port Antonio for the shooting.

It turned out to be a highly amusing week, staying at Errol Flynn's Tichfield Hotel with all expenses paid and a few pounds at the end of it into the bargain. We were delighted with all the quiet nonsense that goes on in the background when a picture is being made. Lovers alone on a deserted beach in the moonlight done in broad daylight with little groups of 'prop' men and the like shooting craps behind every bush, while a couple of yards from the lovers a man with a walkie-talkie sits signalling wildly to the dame to cheat a little.

In the story Ray Milland is the skipper of the schooner and Arlene Dahl is the heroine. Right at the end, where they sail out into the sunset, sitting on the stern of the boat, if you look closely you will notice that the girl is Colin with a red wig on. I wonder if he will ever live that one down.

But soon it was over and back we went to Port Royal to rejoin our own ship and sail off for the Isle of Pines, which lies off the south coast of Cuba. It was blowing the usual gale as we sailed out through the narrow south channel between all the outlying rocks and reefs. Then, when we were half-way through, a local squall came down, bringing the total wind force up to something quite spectacular.

For half-an-hour we had rather a hectic time holding our own

171

against all that wind and keeping our little boat from being blown on to the rocks; then it passed over and we were away, running down past the western end of Jamaica to take our departure for the Isle of Pines.

For the last time we were bowling along before the trade winds together, for Colin would have to leave the ship at the Isle of Pines to fly to Bermuda, if he was to be there in time for the Transatlantic Race to England. I would have to carry on from there to New York alone, unless I could pick up a crew on the way.

It was sad to think that after all those thousands of miles he would not be able to come any further, but at the moment our chief concern was to make good time to the Isle of Pines, for he would have only a few days in hand to get from there to Bermuda to catch his new ship.

My eye was healing nicely. Just before we had left Jamaica we had been offered a lift into town by a friend with an MG. He already had the windshield laid flat and the mast of his sailing boat laid along the length of the car, taking it home, so he and Colin sat in the cockpit while I sat astride the mast on the back.

As we shot out of the boatyard we passed under a bar-taut steel cable which ran across the road about five feet in the air. That is to say, they did. I caught it over the right eye and found myself on my back with large quantities of blood around. Fortunately, however, the driver was a surgeon so he drove us around to the hospital where he gave me a large whisky and sewed it up, using neither anaesthetic nor antiseptic of any kind.

Patrick has the most amazing luck. The most awful things happen to him, but he gets away with them.

And now it was healing up beautifully, leaving hardly a scar from what had been a sizeable gash. Good stuff, whisky.

We sailed through the Cayman Islands without seeing any of them. When we were among them they were about thirty miles away each side of us. We could see quite clearly where they were by the thin lines of white cumulus clouds that always form over land on a hot day, but we never came close enough to make out the islands themselves.

A couple more days of good downwind sailing and the low, wooded coast of the Isle of Pines appeared like a thick, black pencil mark on the horizon ahead. Closing in, we felt our way carefully along the reef, looking for the beacon that marks the gap. Then, just as we approached it, down came a real witches' brew of a storm, full of thunder and lightning and wind and rain.

It passed right over us and near the middle it was blowing so strongly that, although we had taken all the sail off her, *Sopranino* was heeling right over under the pressure of the wind on her bare mast, while the rain and spray were driving so hard that we could not look into it at all.

For perhaps twenty minutes we lay there, just off the reef, the wind fairly screeching in the rigging and all the world a uniform flat grey of flying water. Then as suddenly as it had come it passed over, leaving us becalmed, rolling and slatting on a heavy oily swell.

Then down came the darkness. We could not attempt that tricky entrance to a strange and little-used harbour in the dark, so all night we beat to and fro, working our way in as close to the reefs as we dared, waiting for our chance to enter the lagoon and wondering if Colin would ever catch his plane to Bermuda.

In the morning we slipped through the gap in the reefs, to sail the thirty-odd miles round the island inside the reefs to Nueva Gerona, the only port. By the time we arrived there it was dark again, and once more we had to lie to for the night. One more day had gone by and still we were not in.

But one thing we did do. We spotted the tiny light that marks the entrance and got our bearings on it, so that when the dawn came up we were able to run in towards it.

The Isle of Pines is the oddest shape—round and flat as a gigantic gramophone record, with half-a-dozen steep little mountains sticking up here and there on it. But the mountains are some distance inshore, and the coast itself is, for the most part, just one long, wavy line of dense mangrove swamps.

Sopranino

The entrance to Nueva Gerona is practically invisible until you are almost on top of it, but we found a likely-looking line of stakes and followed these as they twisted and turned to mark the winding channel over the mud flats to where it suddenly curves in between the mangroves and becomes a narrow, muddy river through the swamps.

Inside we were out of the wind, behind the trees. Slowly we drifted over the dark smooth waters of the river with practically no feeling of motion at all. We might well have been up any lonely jungle river a thousand miles from the sea.

There was no sign of any kind of life there at all and we began to wonder whether we had come to the right place. But one or two large fishing boats came gliding past us, their high sails catching the wind over the trees, so we followed them up the winding river. We crept past a shack, then another, to round a bend and find a bridge ahead, with half-a-dozen houses and a few shacks on our right and a cluster of fishing boats moored against a grassy bank on our left. We had arrived at Nueva Gerona.

My goodness—the mosquitoes in Nueva Gerona. They take pride in biting through four layers of clothing. The crickets, too, are full size. As we sailed up the creek, we thought there must be a factory somewhere, by the din that was going on: a high, screeching whine, something between a bandsaw and an electric drill. But it was the crickets.

A large portly gentleman in military uniform, with a gun on his belt, came down to where we were moored to a decrepit little landing stage, and announced in voluble Cuban that he was the customs officer. We agreed pleasantly, but that did not seem to pacify him. It seems that our studies of Spanish had not been very effective, for we had quite a time until an interpreter was summoned to help us explain who we were and what we were doing in his port.

However all was finally settled and after lunch we were allowed ashore to walk up the dusty road to the main street of the town, one long straight street that looked just like the setting for a Western movie, complete with men in large hats lolling against the buildings with guns on their hips.

Westward to Cuba

We found that the plane for Havana and the outside world left in the morning, so Colin got his ticket and we had a farewell dinner in the back yard of a small restaurant before returning home for our last night aboard *Sopranino*.

Up early to a frenzy of packing and last-minute arrangements, cut short by the ancient taxi calling to take us to the airport. Out we went, rattling over the rough road through the fields to the top of a rise, where it came to a dead end at a hut about twenty feet square. The airport.

Through the hut lay a grass field with a twin-engined aircraft loading up for the flight to Havana. Colin turned in the doorway:

'Well, thanks for the buggy ride.'

'Not at all. Come for a sail again some day', I said, as he gathered up his sack of clothes and went out to board the plane.

A last wave, the slam of the door, a roar from the engines and she was off, rising into the air over the rolling fields. I stood and watched as the plane dwindled to a dot on the horizon, then turned to walk slowly back down the long dusty road towards *Sopranino*, alone.

CHAPTER ELEVEN

Florida Reefs

*Patrick Finds a Crew—Waterspouts and Thunderstorms—A Bombing Target—
The Crew Goes Home—Patrick Sails Alone—Nearly Wrecked on the Florida Reefs—
Sopranino Arrives in Miami—The Police and the Blonde—Ethalion Collected—
Inland Waterway—The Dismal Swamp—Chesapeake and Delaware—New York*

A s I came back to the boat I remembered Colin's words out at the airport, just before he left:

'This is a hell of a place to leave a man'.

Too true. Miles up a dirty, lonely creek in a foreign land where very few people understood English. But he couldn't help it. All these things had been arranged months ago. And now I had work to do: sail *Sopranino* three hundred miles around the end of Cuba to Havana, then another two hundred to Miami, then get my visa and take her up 1200 miles of inland waterway to New York.

But first the run to Havana. For this I decided that some sort of crew would be advisable, as it might easily take some time and we should be in the shipping lanes all the way.

After a certain amount of hunting around I found two young local boys who spoke English and were prepared to come, though neither of them had ever been out of the harbour in a boat in his life. So far, so good.

But then the customs officer put his spoke in. It was unthinkable, he said, that the boys should sail off in a foreign boat without a Permit. I asked, what permit? That he didn't know, but this was something unusual and for things unusual you've got to have a Permit.

This looked like becoming something of an impasse. I had very little money and it wouldn't last long where I was. Certainly I couldn't afford to fly to Havana for a nebulous permit. Meanwhile there I was, stuck. Bureaucrats, bah!

Then I had an idea. There was a radio-telephone to Havana.

Florida Reefs

I inquired where it was, and was directed across a grassy field to a gay little shack in the centre of a fine cluster of tall, spindly aerials waving precariously in the breeze.

Inside sat a charming young woman surrounded by strange devices that howled like banshees whenever she touched them. After much sign language we got through to Havana, and finally to the good Colin, who promised to see what could be done at that end.

He had been held up by some technical complication, which was lucky for me as he was able to see the right person and have a message sent ordering the customs officer to release the boys, the boat, and me. In fact if Colin had not been there I might never have got away and would have probably become a Cuban farmer by now.

But as it was we gathered some food and water aboard, bade our farewells and sailed down the narrow river and out to sea once more, bound for Havana.

The 150-odd miles down to Cape San Antonio, the most western point of Cuba, was fairly easy going, with light, following winds all the way. The two boys soon settled in, taking it in turns to steer the courses I gave them, while I navigated, cooked, and did everything else.

Then, off the Cape, we found the most tiresome weather. A series of thunderstorms, with much lightning and sharp little winds from every direction in them. When you were in one you would be rushing at high speed in a totally undesirable direction, hanging on and hoping that you would not be struck by the lightning. Then suddenly you would be out of that one, drifting aimlessly around in circles until the next one came.

Another speciality they have there is waterspouts. Huge columns of water, maybe six feet or more around and rising hundreds of feet into the air to disappear in a dark cloud, they would move slowly across the water, snaking and twisting as they went.

I should hate to think what would happen if one hit a small boat such as ours. Water is heavy stuff and those spouts were spinning fast. Furthermore, they have a strong tendency to take things up with them. So presumably either they would churn you up like a gigantic mincing machine or you would find yourself suddenly at a great height. And about the only items of equipment that we did not have on board was parachutes, so we made a point of staying away from them.

The boys, who had lived around these parts all their lives, were not particularly impressed. On one occasion I pointed out four of the things in sight at one time. They agreed that when they did hit small boats they usually tore them apart, but said that it did not happen often and anyway that was the weather and there it was.

Apparently these waterspouts are hollow in the middle, the water being drawn upward by the vacuum effect. If, then, you can break the wall of the thing and release the vacuum it will collapse comparatively harmlessly. The trick, the boys said, was to wait until it got within about six feet of you and then stick an oar into it and hang on tight. With its own spinning motion it would tear a hole in itself on the blade of the oar, the air would rush in, and the whole thing would collapse.

But little by little we worked our way through that area, to stand out from the shore into better weather for the run up to Havana. The only trouble was that out there the wind was too light, drifting us along at about one knot, barely twenty-four miles a day, while closer inshore we could see the thunder and lightning every afternoon, as regular as clockwork, from four o'clock until sundown.

After a couple of days of drifting around like that we ran out of water. It was entirely my own fault, for I had grown careless on so many comparatively short journeys and no longer bothered to check our supplies regularly. The boys were not used to rationing it; the weather was calm and very hot; we had taken longer than I had estimated. All these things together had combined to leave us some thirty miles offshore, becalmed under the tropical sun, with barely a couple of days' water left.

We immediately went into strict rationing and began to drift in towards the Cuban coast, looking for a nice thunderstorm. Next afternoon we got one—first wind, around the edge of it, then a teeming rainstorm in the middle. I set up the mainsail to catch the rain, dashing about putting cooking pots under the corner where it ran off, and inside twenty minutes we had six quarts; two more days' supply, if we were careful.

Closer to the coast the going was faster, if a little hectic, and two days later the city of Havana came shimmering through the haze across the wide yellow sweep of the bay ahead of us.

Eagerly we pointed *Sopranino's* nose at it, but it was not to be that easy. A naval motor launch came fussing over to tell us to stand clear of the harbour. It was the Fourth of July and they were having a dive-bombing display by way of celebration. So off we drifted, over towards the coast, to wait for them to stop.

Late in the afternoon the planes seemed to have all gone home, so we nosed on across the bay towards the entrance. Half-way across there was a roar behind us and another squadron turned up, laden with large sand-filled bombs intended for the target that looked just like a small sailing boat, over to the east of us. Hurriedly we dropped all our sails and waved enthusiastically until they had all passed over, then up went our sails and on we went. This game went on, with variations, for the rest of the afternoon, until finally they did go home and we could continue on into the harbour.

It was around midnight when we finally drifted through the long straight entrance—past floodlit hotels and restaurants while cars rushed madly up and down the road beside us, their horns blaring—and made fast to the jetty of the International Yacht Club.

Early in the morning the boys went off home, leaving me to look around for a crew for the next hop, to Miami, two hundred miles away. I spent four days wandering around the various magnificent yacht clubs without any luck. The yacht clubs really are magnificent, in the true sense of the word. Vast palatial buildings with great courtyards, several hundred feet across, looking out over the sea. There, those who like to do their sailing in comfort can sit under the shade of coloured umbrellas while well-trained waiters bring them drinks.

Sopranino

I could not waste any more time or money there, so I went back to the boat. I would have to make the next passage alone and that was that. A large black big-game fishing boat came in and tied up alongside, and a big rugged-looking type came over to introduce himself:

'My name's Hemingway. Come and have a drink.'

It was Ernest Hemingway, who lives out in the country near Havana and keeps his boat at the dock for fishing trips. We had a very pleasant and rather alcoholic evening and next morning I prepared to leave for Miami. The show must go on.

I had heard that the Gulf Stream was kicking up a bit just then, but outside I found nothing unusual, beyond the ordinary seas five or six feet high, as I laid my course to the northward towards the American coast.

There was a fair amount of wind and it looked as though there might soon be more, so as soon as we were twenty-five miles offshore I snugged her down a little, set the automatic steering gear and retired below to get some sleep, leaving *Sopranino* to work her way up to windward on her own.

All the next day it blew good and hard against us, while every couple of hours a nasty little squall would come down to add to the general discomfort. Even when we were hove-to and not moving the wind was really howling in the rigging and some of the gusts were laying *Sopranino* down, shaking her like a dog with a rat.

After dark I identified the American Shoals lighthouse, standing guard on the long line of reefs that runs parallel to the low, sandy coast about five miles off. A busy evening was spent dodging ships as we bounced over the short, steep seas and out to seaward again, off the shipping lanes, for the night.

The following morning the sky was overcast with low grey clouds, as it had been all the previous day, so there was no chance of fixing our position by the sun. It was still blowing good and hard, and every hour or so a thundersquall would come down, blotting out all visibility and forcing me to take in the only sail I had up.

Each time this happened we would be forced back towards

the dangerous reefs. Then, as it eased, I would have to come out, set the mainsail, and work my way out against it for a mile or two, ready for the next squall. This routine went on all day, and very tiresome it was. The scrambled eggs for lunch did not need any shaking. The problem was to persuade them to stay in the pot.

By four in the afternoon I still had not been able to fix our position; we were closing in towards the coast again and, what with the Gulf Stream and the squalls, I was by no means certain where we were. If you strike the coast in that area at night and in clear weather it is quite easy, as the lighthouses are so spaced that you are almost bound to see one of them; but in daylight and in poor visibility those reefs can be extremely dangerous, as the large number of wrecked ships marked on the chart testifies only too graphically.

The reefs mostly lie five miles or so from the low shore, so that you would strike them before you saw the land. They are very steep, coming right up almost to the surface. Obviously if you were to strike one in a little boat with a strong wind blowing on to the shore it would mean almost certain death, for the boat would break up in a matter of minutes, pounded on the sharp coral by the waves.

We were sailing along, *Sopranino* and I, closing the coast in the hope of picking up a light as it got dark and thus fix our position. The sea was deep blue and since I had seen no ships for some time it looked as though we still had some way to go, so I decided to go down into the cabin for a few minutes to try and get a bearing on the radio direction-finder.

This is kept well forward in the cabin, out of the way of any spray, and to use it you have to crawl forward in your bunk, lying on your side to reach the controls. For a while I fiddled with the thing without much result, then suddenly I decided to go up on deck and have a look around.

When I got up in the hatch I looked over the side and said to myself:

'What pretty green water . . . *green!*' That means only one thing—reefs. Then I looked around, and there was a day

Sopranino

beacon a couple of hundred yards away, to seaward! We were over a reef; which one, I could not be certain. It might have been any one of two or three so I had no clue as to the best way off it again. And there, bearing down on us, was a stinker of a thundersquall.

The situation was rapidly getting out of hand and quick action was called for. There was only one thing to do: sail out the way we had come in and hope for the best. The wind was coming up rapidly. The boat would never come about against it, so we would have to run off before it and swing around that way. I slammed over the tiller, let go the main sheet, and off we swung.

Down came the rain, blotting out visibility to zero, and with it the full force of the storm. Time only for a quick glance at the compass to get a bearing for the run out, then it caught her. It hit *Sopranino* so hard that she would not come about for a moment, but rushed madly off for the middle of the reef, gathering speed rapidly.

I grabbed a length of line, tied the tiller hard over, rushed forward, and hauled down half the mainsail. For a moment she hovered, running straight before the storm with the reef flashing past just under her keel. Any moment she might strike —and that would be that.

Then slowly she swung round in a great arc over the boiling seas. The mainsail came over with a bang. I hoisted it up again, then went back to release the tiller, set our course, and run out. As suddenly as it came, the storm passed over. We were in deep blue water again, with the beacon dropping away behind us.

Out in the Gulf Stream the weather continued to be unkind, with the fierce little squalls every hour or so. I began to think that this was the normal weather around those parts, until I arrived in Miami to find that it had been logged as a storm of fifty miles an hour and more all along the coast. The warning signals are put up for a wind of twenty-five miles an hour, half that.

Two days later we arrived at Miami, only to find the tide

running out so fast through the entrance that we could not get in. For five hours we lay rolling to the anchor before the tide turned and swept us in between the breakwaters.

Inside, all was calm and peaceful. Slowly we sailed down past the long MacArthur Causeway, watching all the cars rushing to and fro in the strong morning sunlight, to dock in at the Municipal Yacht Basin. Up went the little American flag. We were there at last. Over ten months and seven thousand miles out of Falmouth.

A couple of days spent seeing the customs, immigration, health, and other authorities, between press interviews and radio and television shows, and I was ready to take *Sopranino* up the river to leave her where she would be safe from hurricanes while I flew to Nassau to get my own personal papers cleared.

I was docked right next to the police launch. One morning when I awoke late, after a party the night before, the police announced that a beautiful blonde in a blue coupé had called, asking for me. They had said I was out, so after waiting for an hour she had gone away. I asked them for her telephone number. They hadn't got it, or any means of contacting her. I never did find out who she was, but I had a lot of fun kidding the police boys about it.

Finally, by way of atonement, they gave me a tow with their launch up the river, through the town with its seven bridges, to a safe dock where I could leave *Sopranino* while I was away.

An hour's flight took me to Nassau, where for seven weeks I stayed aboard a luxurious 47-foot auxiliary yacht called *Ethalion*, as the guest of her owner, Gerald Ross, while I waited for my American visa to come through.

It was a wonderful rest, though an enforced one, after the long haul through all the islands. A few weeks before I had been stuck, almost penniless, in a remote and dirty creek in the Isle of Pines. Now for nearly two months I was to enjoy the luxury of a cabin nearly eight feet square, where I could catch up with my writing and my correspondence. There was

Sopranino

enough money to have a meal or a drink in town occasionally and enjoy for a brief while the everyday luxuries of a civilised life.

But it was not to last. There was plenty of work to be done before we should reach New York. The papers were completed, the visa came through, and I was ready to be on my way once more.

Taking *Sopranino* up through a thousand miles of narrow, sheltered inland waterway was going to be a problem. I was thinking that one over when Gerald Ross announced that he wanted *Ethalion* taken to Annapolis, on Chesapeake Bay. He offered to fill her up with fuel and pay all dockages due on her if I would run her up for him. This was ideal for me, as with her motor I could take both boats through the rivers and canals as far as Chesapeake Bay and sort the matter out from there.

Just then Hurricane Able had passed by, and Baker, the second one, was on its way towards Nassau. Whether or not it would hit the island was uncertain, but it was coming straight for it, and was about two days off.

If it caught *Ethalion* in Nassau harbour it would finish her off, so I decided to start at once, reckoning that if I kept going fast to the westward I could keep clear ahead of it and get her up Miami Canal to safety, before it caught up with us.

We dashed round in Gerald's car, clearing customs and the various other authorities. We found a Negro boy to come with me as crew as far as Miami, and loaded up the boat with supplies of tinned goods to last me through the weeks ahead.

Late that night the latest report on the hurricane came in; it was closing in, moving straight towards us. I spoke to the harbour master.

'What speed can you make under power?' he asked.

'Seven knots', I said.

'Well, if you leave right away and your motor doesn't stop, you should make it.'

At midnight we motored out past the town, down the line of buoys blinking in the darkness, and out to sea. Three hours later, when we were somewhere among the reefs twenty miles

Florida Reefs

from Nassau, the motor faltered and died, leaving us creeping along at a couple of knots in the light breeze.

At that rate it would take us seventy hours to cover the 140-odd miles between us and Miami. Three days. Long before that the hurricane could catch us up. Something would have to be done, and soon.

I prised up the floorboards to peer at the engine with the aid of a flashlight. Below me was a hot, oily, smelly mass of machinery, silent and inert. I tried the starter hopefully. Nothing happened. I looked across at the boy:

'Keep her as she is, will you, for a moment, while I just fix this thing.' I tried to sound confident, though to tell the truth I had never used that make of engine before and had not the least idea what might be the matter with it.

Still, it was a motor, and motors have to have fuel, so I undid the pipe. Nothing came out. There was a complicated mass of filters, cleaners, and pipes leading away into the darkness in all directions. Slowly, little by little, I traced from the tank through all the filters to the engine. No blockages. I sounded the tank. Plenty of fuel there. I strolled casually up on deck under the watchful eye of the boy sitting at the wheel, lit a cigarette, and sat down to think this thing out.

Then I had an idea. The tank was *below* the engine. Therefore it must suck its fuel *up*. So the least air leak and it wouldn't get any. Back I went below, to check over all the joints, blowing and sucking down the various lengths of piping and getting mouthfuls of sickly Diesel oil, until at last it came out of the right place.

When I had finished being sick I tried the starter:

'Whirr. Whirr!' Silence. I tried again.

'Whirr. Herumph!' and a puff of smoke. Then again.

'Herumph, Herumph!' and two puffs of smoke.

I crossed my fingers and gave it one more try. It fired, picked up and settled down to a steady throb, sending us surging forward again over the calm swells towards Miami.

Soon it was light, and all that day the motor kept going, rumbling away below the floor as we picked our way between the thousands of tiny islands, across the shallow flats. Just as it got dark we slid out into the Gulf Stream and by morning we were in Miami.

Ashore we found that the hurricane had swung off to the northward, so that we should hardly feel it where we were, so I settled down to the business of clearing with the different authorities. The immigration people were rather alarming about my Negro boy. His papers as a seaman were quite in order, but I had to see him on the plane home within forty-eight hours or I would find myself responsible for a heavy fine.

He was a nice quiet boy and he explained that he wanted to go ashore in the evening to see his aunt. That seemed reasonable enough, so I explained the position and told him to make sure and be back by seven in the morning, and went about my business.

In the morning there was no sign of him. Eight, nine, ten o'clock. Still no sign. I reported to the police. They looked cheerful, gloating a little after the kidding I had been giving them over the blonde they let slip:

'We have a nice cell that's just your size'. Then, more help-fully:

'Try the town jail; he probably got drunk'.

Down I went to the jail and there he was. He had had a lovely evening, got roaring drunk and into a fight, and spent the night in the jail, where he was now sitting waiting to come up before the court.

It was nice to find him, anyway. Soon I had him bailed out and I clung on to him like a leech until I saw him into his plane and the plane off the ground. Then, with a sigh of relief, I went back to cope with my own problems.

First I had to take the big boat, *Ethalion*, up the river. Then I hooked *Sopranino* on behind her and her dinghy on behind that and set out, with an old set of out-of-date charts, to navigate the thousand miles of canals, rivers, and inland lakes to Chesapeake Bay.

All through Florida we chuffed, day after day, down long

straight canals, sometimes in a channel only thirty yards wide with a mile of shallow water either side of us, but more often through lonely swamps and marshes, with nothing in sight but dense tangled mangroves and muddy water.

It was not practical to run in the dark alone with three boats to look after, so each evening at dusk I would have to find a dock or some little creek where I could pull in for the night and secure the whole brood.

Then, in the morning, I would be up before daybreak, sorting them all out for the day's run, and all day I would be on the wheel with the chart and the binoculars, finding our way through canals and creeks, through busy towns and wild marshes, under innumerable bridges.

With *Ethalion's* tall masts we had to have each bridge opened before we could go through it. And there were all kinds of bridges: bridges that opened upward in one or in two parts; bridges that swung around; bridges that rose slowly into the air on great towers. There were even some gay little bridges that broke into pieces that swung around on their own individual axes.

In fact it got to the point where I hardly dared blow my hooter for fear that one of them would disintegrate or disappear in a puff of smoke.

Then they had dredgers. Massive things as big as a small block of flats, sitting squarely in the middle of the channel, covered with cranes and surrounded by tugs and barges.

The first time I encountered one of these it seemed impossible that we should ever get past it. However, I gave a tiny experimental squeak on my hooter, whereupon there was a hooting and a tooting and a clanging and a banging, and the whole bag of tricks sidled out of the channel, to collapse with a hiss like a punctured haggis.

As the days stretched into weeks we came into Georgia, swirling up and down winding rivers on the strong tides, across open sounds, and up more rivers. There we had our next hurricane warning that sent us scurrying into a noisome dock, laying out lines in all directions to hold each boat safely if it

should strike. But it passed by off the coast, so out we came and on up into the Carolinas.

There they had barges. Huge things lashed together in fours loaded with logs for the paper mills. They would come swinging around a corner ahead of us, sweeping the channel like a gigantic windscreen wiper. And of course the logs fell off, so that all the time I had to be on the lookout for great hunks of timber floating in the water that could bend the propeller on the big boat or knock a hole in the bottom of the little ones.

At last we reached the Dismal Swamp. I had been given a Sopranino flute for my birthday, and had picked this spot out as the ideal place to practise playing it. But it was not to be, for when we arrived there the canal through it was empty and the swamp itself was on fire. So we went around the other way to Norfolk, Virginia, and out into Chesapeake Bay.

There we docked in at Hampton, just across from Norfolk, with another thousand miles behind us and only three hundred-odd to go to New York. But all the boats were dirty and messy after their long trail through the waterways, so I spent five or six weeks, single-handed, cleaning and painting each one in turn before running *Ethalion* up to Annapolis and turning her over to the yard there.

To save a little time, Ray Brown, a young Coast Guard officer, and I took his 30-foot motorboat and towed *Sopranino* up Chesapeake Bay, through the Chesapeake and Delaware Canal and down the Delaware River to Cape May, where we left her, ready for the final run up to New York.

He had to report back to duty, so he left me to bring his boat back to Hampton. Three days later I was chugging back down Chesapeake Bay, approaching Norfolk. It was Christmas Eve and I was tired after seven days of almost continuous running. The visibility had closed right in, it was dark, and I was feeling lonely and depressed out there in the wide bay with only a chart and a compass to go by.

Then a large steamer came along, moving slowly in the fog. Obviously he must be going to Norfolk, I thought, so I plugged in behind him and followed him on in.

Sopranino

As we entered the harbour there seemed to be something strange about it, but I put that down to the fog and the general depression. Then, as we got inside, it quite obviously wasn't Norfolk. It turned out to be some remote little port I had never heard of, so out I went and continued on around to Hampton, docking in the early hours of Christmas morning.

By way of celebration I had a good sleep, to wake around midday and find my shoes floating past my face. The little motorboat had decided to do a sinking act. I switched on the electric pump. It didn't work. It wasn't in the mood. So with much bad language I put the sea back in its place outside, tidied the boat up, and handed her back to her owner.

Now to get back to *Sopranino* in Cape May. There I was lucky. Ray's brother had a light aircraft and was on leave, so off we went, bumping and bouncing merrily over the fields of Virginia and Delaware, to land near the docks. With a roar and a wave they were away, leaving me once more alone in *Sopranino*, this time on a bitterly cold wind-swept coast, but with only another 150 miles to New York.

The quickest route would have been outside, straight up the coast, but alone and with no stove, with the temperature going down to 15 degrees below freezing at nights and strong north-easterly gales sweeping down against one every few days, it would have been taking an unnecessary risk. One might have succumbed to the cold and exhaustion and lost control of the boat.

So for the next hundred miles I sailed her up the narrow winding waterways to Manasquan Inlet, where they finished. It was interesting to do a section of waterway under sail, though it was a slow and messy process, beating back and forth up the long narrow cuts.

At Manasquan I stopped for a couple of days, checking over *Sopranino's* gear and preparing for the final forty-mile run up the Jersey coast. And on the morning of January 6, sixteen months to a day since we had left England, we were ready. The weather forecast was fair. This was it.

For the last time we put our noses out of a harbour, to sail out on to the heaving ocean. She heeled to the fresh northerly breeze as the inlet faded away behind us, dancing over the waves past the bare poles of the fish traps that stood gaunt and solitary on the edge of the shallows, into deep water once more.

All day we sailed up within sight of the distant shore, checking off our landmarks on the chart. One by one they came up, the Atlantic Highlands, a single range of hills standing straight up from the low coastline. Scotland Light vessel. And Sandy Hook, flat and yellow, tapering down into the green of the sea.

As the sun went down the wind increased a little, so that I had to lean out over the side to balance *Sopranino* as it caught her and sent her bouncing into the short, steep seas, wisps of spray flying into the air from her bow to freeze in a thin sheet of ice on her sails, while ahead, one by one, the lights of New York came twinkling through the haze.

Epilogue

WHEN *Sopranino* sailed into New York Harbour she had completed some ten thousand miles of sailing, and an idea had become a reality. We had proved that really small boats, properly designed and constructed, are capable of standing up to any weather that they are likely to encounter anywhere on the face of the seas. We had gathered a great deal of information, much of it on small details which, taken together, make up a sum of knowledge that can mean the difference between death by misadventure and a safe return to port for those who follow after us. And we had opened up the possibility, for thousands of young people who cannot afford to buy or to run large seagoing boats, of owning their own little boats in which they can go out on to the wide seas away from the artificial surroundings of modern life, and learn the many things that such an experience has to teach.

The Technical Side

The Boat — Equipment — Handling — Navigation — Preparation — Organization
—Stores—Colin's Second Thoughts—Some Special Skills for Sopranauts

THE BOAT

WHEN considering the specifications for a boat which is intended to operate in the open sea it is important not to lose sight of the basic essentials. A boat is a thing for floating on the water in. If it ceases to float its occupants will probably drown. Therefore, first and foremost, it must be so constructed that it cannot sink, whatever happens to it.

Most small boats, if filled with water, will promptly sink. Some that are claimed to be unsinkable have buoyancy tanks or bags, which help. But if these are punctured in an accident the boat still sinks. This is not good enough.

In *Sopranino* the first requirement was that she should be literally unsinkable. This was achieved by constructing her as lightly as possible, consistent with adequate strength, and fitting into her a sufficient quantity of Onazote (an expanded rubber material) to float her, together with her keel, her crew, and all her gear and stores, plus a reserve of 250 pounds.

Onazote has a constant lift, when submerged, of nearly sixty pounds per cubic foot. It comes in solid blocks and you can stick a knife in it or break it up into chunks without its losing any appreciable buoyancy. Thus *Sopranino* would always continue to float and to support her crew, even if she were filled with water and crushed into a ball.

Secondly, a seagoing boat must be self-righting; that is to say, if she were turned completely upside down with her keel straight up in the air, she would turn herself the right way up again without any assistance.

This was achieved by making *Sopranino* almost circular in

Sopranino

section amidships and fitting her with a fin keel having a bulb of lead on it. Thus, if she were inverted—filled or empty—the centre of gravity would always be above the centre of buoyancy. The force of gravity could be relied upon to do the rest.

These requirements are, of course, far more stringent than those of any other type of boat or ship afloat, including lifeboats, but we were aiming for the ideal condition and as far as these basic premises were concerned, we got it.

Next, it was considered highly desirable that she should not fill unless actually holed. To achieve this the after hatch was bedded on rubber and screwed down at sea, while the only other opening in the ship was the main hatch, located as centrally as possible and as high as possible.

This was kept to the smallest size consistent with easy and rapid egress by the crew and was fitted with a hinged lifting cover, to insure that the crew could never be trapped inside, unable to get out.

The cockpit was a watertight box, having the minimum practicable volume, fitted with a drain to the sea, tapered to reduce the area of the opening, and located well forward in the vessel so that when filled the weight would not unduly upset her trim.

The specification called for the mast and rigging to be so designed that they would stand the strain imposed by the boat's being rolled clean over with all sail up in a storm at sea. This quality is hard to prove, though I have seen the tall racing mast hit the water with a bang during a gale off the Spanish coast without showing the slightest ill effects, and the shorter cruising mast is appreciably stronger.

Furthermore, the strains imposed on the mast and rigging are in general a function of the mass and the righting moment of the boat, so that in the case of an extremely small and light boat they are vastly less than those to be expected in similar conditions in the previous accepted types of seagoing sailing boats.

The extremely light weight (the hull, when built, only weighed 410 pounds) provided considerable advantages.

The Technical Side

Ashore it rendered her easy to handle and, together with the use of a detachable fin, made it possible to trail her behind a normal car and store her in the garage for the winter. While at sea it enormously reduced the strains imposed on her and at the same time gave her such a high ratio of potential lift to running weight that she always rode lightly and easily over the tops of the waves, however large and awkward, without suffering any harm.

The small size and light weight of her sails and gear made her very easy to handle, particularly in heavy weather, giving an effect similar to that which would be achieved in more normal-sized boats if the members of their crews were, say, twelve feet tall.

On top of these basic advantages over previously accepted standards, the most careful attention was paid to every detail, to ensure that it would be as efficient as possible. This policy was probably pursued to even greater lengths than the most highly developed ocean racing yachts in the world today have yet achieved.

As examples: She carried three compasses, none of them having any errors whatever; a complete range of tools and spares, right down to spare planks, and usually a skilled boatbuilder to fit them; and two separate cooking stoves, independent of each other.

The result was that she was an extremely efficient sea boat in every way. In fact it may reasonably be said that she was one of the safest vessels of any kind that has ever floated on the sea.

EQUIPMENT

For racing or local cruising within a radius of around five hundred miles from home *Sopranino* carried her tall racing mast, some twenty-seven feet high, with upper and lower spreaders. Under this rig she was a cutter, carrying twin headsails, following the practice of many modern ocean racers.

Her sails consisted of: Mainsail, Masthead Genoa, Number

Sopranino

One Jib, Number Two Jib, Genoa Staysail, Number One Staysail, Masthead Spinnaker, and Storm Trysail.

For long-distance and ocean cruising she carried a stouter mast, some six feet shorter, having wide single spreaders and a sloop sail plan: Mainsail, Genoa Jib, Number One Jib, Trysail, and Twin Spinnakers.

The cruising mainsail was specially designed by Ratsey. It had neither headboard nor battens and was cut with a gore from the clew to a point halfway up the luff, with cloths running parallel to the leach and foot. This was a great success, arriving in the United States showing practically no signs of chafe or wear at all.

The twin spinnakers were of heavy nylon in contrast to all the other sails which were of normal canvas. They were set like jibs, hanked on to twin forestays and cut very high indeed, which proved to be very necessary in view of the considerable rolling that was experienced in the trade winds.

They had their own twin booms, which were originally pivoted on the foredeck but later transferred to a point about six feet up the mast with greatly improved results, and by leading the guys aft *via* blocks to the tiller we were able to make the boat steer herself before the wind satisfactorily for weeks on end.

The storm trysail we never in fact used in all our travels, thought it was nice to have it around. We also carried oil bags and an eight-foot Voss-type sea anchor but never found the need for them.

A battened sun awning that was set over the boom in port in the tropics proved to be an essential item. Without it the heat in port, with no cooling breezes, would have been definitely excessive.

In case we should ever lose the use of our rudder, a blade was carried that could be attached to either of the spinnaker booms and mounted in a rowlock on the stern as an auxiliary steering device. This also served for propulsion over short distances when we were becalmed.

Our racing anchor was a $3\frac{1}{2}$-pound Danforth. The use of this

The Technical Side

was based on the theory that it would be for kedging in calms only, since in port we should moor and at sea we should never place ourselves in a position where we should have to rely on an anchor as a safety device.

For cruising, however, we carried a seventeen-pounder C.Q.R., with two fathoms of chain and some forty fathoms of warp. The chain, besides greatly improving the holding power of the anchor itself, is absolutely necessary for anchoring in the vicinity of coral, which can cut through the ordinary warp in very little time.

The warp was of grass rope, for lightness. It also made an excellent drogue if required, for running before a heavy storm. All other ropes and lines were of Italian hemp and stood up excellently to the long hard wear that they received.

Both the racing and the cruising mainsails, by the way, were fitted with old-fashioned reef points, thereby allowing the use of a flat boom on which were fitted a main sheet lead to the forward end of the cockpit, clew outhaul, and standing topping lift. For trade wind sailing the boom was clamped in position by two aluminium alloy struts aft, to serve as a handhold during the heavy rolling.

For cruising in tropical waters under the short rig, an aluminium guard rail about a foot above the deck was fitted all around the after portion of the vessel, with a canvas dodger round it. This provided us with a large and comfortable deck space secure from the attention of passing sharks.

On the foredeck a stainless steel wire, covered with plastic tubing, was fitted three inches above deck level. This acted both as a handrail and as a toe hold, proving very effective at sea. In addition, a personal life-line, attached to the mast or to the guard rail, was always worn around the waist by any member of the crew on deck.

The ordinary racing flag or club burgee wears out after continuous use in heavy weather, in about two weeks, so we used an eighteen-inch wind sock that remained at the masthead for over a year without showing any appreciable signs of wear. For use in port a complete set of the flags of the various countries to be visited was carried, together with the Red Ensign, club burgees, and the flags P and Q of the International Code.

Our fenders were interesting—pneumatic, weighing only a few ounces each, and deflating for stowage.

The automatic steering gear, our own adaptation of the well-known Braine Gear used in model yachts, was well worth its weight, being particularly useful when one was single-handed or when one of us wanted to go forward and do something while the other was asleep. But for a gear of this type to work well it is necessary to ensure that the rudder always swings freely and smoothly.

Below, the two bunks were six feet six inches long and rather narrow, padded with sponge rubber covered in plastic, each forming a deep U-shaped trough in which one can sleep in the roughest weather without any fear of being thrown out.

Dorade-type watertrap ventilators were fitted with their standpipes located over the bunks, so that the incoming air flowed past the face of the man sleeping, through the galley, and out of the ventilation slot below the hatch. The hatch itself was fitted with a Perspex panel for viewing the sails from inside the cabin.

The lighting system was twelve-volt electric. There were two unspillable batteries, designed for aerobatic aircraft, from which were run interior lights over the chart table, galley, and bunks, plus compass light, combination red and green running light, and white thirty-two-point masthead light.

This last item proved over and over again to be highly efficient for the vital task of making one's position known to steamers, and rates as one of the most essential pieces of equipment in a small seagoing boat. Another obvious one is a good pump and, although we had one mounted in the cabin for use from inside if necessary, we never had enough water in the ship to use it; we removed the little we had daily with a sponge.

On the subject of lights, we did try a wind generator, but discarded it as we found that the wind strength at low levels in a seaway varied so much that the thing would never deliver current at a constant rate.

The Technical Side

The twin cooking stoves were made up out of Primus parts working on the pressure paraffin principle, with deep galleries fitting the pots and flame and draught guards on three sides. These were made entirely of brass as they were situated within three feet of the main compass.

All plates, cups, and saucers were of lightweight plastic materials, the flexible variety proving most useful. And for protection against marauders both animal and human we carried machetes, fighting knives, and an automatic pistol.

On the maintenance side, a complete range of tools, materials, and spares was carried, sufficient to enable us to do any repair or replacement on the boat or on any item of her sails, gear, and equipment. This in fact meant a very large number of items—from spare sailcloth in all weights to the right-sized screws for fitting each piece of spare hardware.

The main problem on such a long trip is not that of breakage but of wear and tear, and the action of sun and seawater over long periods. Worms, of course, have to be guarded against most carefully in tropical waters, necessitating a careful examination of the bottom every six weeks for signs of their entry.

But chafe is the worst enemy, particularly in the trade winds where the rolling is violent and continuous for weeks on end. It is necessary to conduct a thorough examination of the ship and all her gear at least weekly under those conditions, while certain obvious things such as the chafe of sails against stays require continuous attention. In fact, out of a crew of two it is a full-time job for one man, skilled in those things, to attend to the maintenance of the vessel and keep her in sound sea-going condition.

HANDLING

These midget offshore racers call for their own handling technique, which is closer to that of a racing dinghy than that of a cruising boat of normal displacement. For one thing the weight of the two-man crew is half of the total ballast, so that

Sopranino

the boat's performance is greatly affected by changes in the positions of the men aboard her.

In this connection it is interesting to notice that, when sailing to windward at a normal angle of heel, a line drawn vertically through the centre of gravity of a man lying in the windward bunk passes outboard of the rail, so that he is in fact providing as much or more righting moment than he would be doing if he were on deck and sitting out over the side.

In addition to which, in his bunk he is offering no windage, so that the really keen racing crew would be quite correct to recline idly in his bunk while going to windward.

When going to windward the waich below always uses the windward bunk, whichever tack the ship may be on; the two bunks are specially constructed to be comfortable under these conditions. This does not in fact normally mean that he will have to change sides in his sleep, as for offshore work you can usually reckon to stay on one tack at least four hours and time the changes of tack to fit in at the changes of watch.

One advantage of this system of always sleeping up in the windward bunk is that one is well away from any spare water that may have found its way below, though in fact none of it ever finds its way into the leeward bunk as the bunk sides themselves are sealed off and made watertight to stop that.

Entering or leaving ports or harbours, *Sopranino* is so small and can turn so rapidly that she can work her way around under sail almost anywhere without difficulty, though in close quarters it is not advisable to set the large masthead genoa or the jib topsail, for if either of these sails is backed by a freak puff of wind it will spin her around onto the other tack before you can do anything about it.

Normally, then, we would sail out under mainsail and genoa staysail only, a thoroughly handy rig, and once clear of the harbour we would set whatever sails the conditions outside called for.

The cutter rig, used for racing, offers a great variety of alternatives in the way of sail layouts, which means that great things can be done, but for serious competition it may take

The Technical Side

even an expert sailor quite a long time to learn just what combination is best for each precise set of conditions.

With the shorter cruising rig, of course, it is quite a different matter. You simply set your two sails, main and jib, in one port and unless something very extreme happens they stay there until you drift up to the dock in the next port. Naturally you don't get there as fast as you would with the racing rig, but it is much easier on the crew and leaves them more time to rest and keep up with the odd jobs, so that as long as their food and water last they can remain up to their peak potential efficiency in case of an emergency.

For normal passages we found the best routine is that which is described earlier in this book, by which each man is given exactly four hours' sleep from the time he actually gets his head down. Once the boat is at least three or four hundred miles offshore and clear of all shipping lanes the self-steering can be set and the ocean routine can be satisfactorily used.

There are two separate methods of setting the automatic steering, one for running and the other for reaching or fetching. For running with twin spinnakers we found it best to set them so that the booms were between five and ten degrees forward of a line drawn at right angles to the direction of the apparent wind. Then the single fore guy could be set up. This starts from the outward end of one boom, runs forward through a block at the stem, back through an eye at the outboard end of the other boom and is made up on a cleat near the inboard end of it. Thus the whole affair can easily be adjusted while in operation and at the same time it leaves the two booms free to swing together and so operate the steering.

The after guys are then led through blocks onto the tiller, where they are made fast. This is the standard basic arrangement used on most boats for this purpose, but in the case of small light boats it is necessary to add further devices to check the tendency to 'hunt' or swing each side of the course set.

First a line is run from the tiller to a cleat each side, limiting its travel to between 10 and 20 degrees each way. Then a strap of about four parts of standard shock cord is attached

Sopranino

each side of the tiller, a light line being led from one around four cleats in the form of a rectangle around the cockpit and back to the other. This is kept under a tension of about sixty pounds and acts as a damper on the tiller. At the same time it can be used as a bias control, for by simply easing the line a quarter of an inch or so around the cleats it can be made to swing the ship a point off its natural course to compensate for temporary variations in the wind direction.

Altogether this system works very satisfactorily. In our case it worked continuously with little attention for nearly three weeks on end, automatically setting the ship back on course each time she was broached right around by an extra-large breaker, and taking such things as surf-riding and planing in its stride.

Then, for windward work or for reaching, when we were under our normal rig of mainsail and one or more headsails, the other gear was used. This consists of an arc set on the top of the rudder post facing aft, and works on the same principle as the Braine Gear on models.

For this, the main sheet is permanently led from a cleat at the forward end of the cockpit, up to the boom, along it, down to the horse and up again, then down to a block just forward of the after hatch, and forward to terminate at a slider on the arc.

When the slider is in the midships position the gear is out of action and in nobody's way. Then when it is wanted one only has to slide it out a few inches to windward until the pull on the main sheet balances the pressure on the rudder and it will take over, keeping the ship at that angle to the apparent wind while the helmsman leaves the tiller to go forward to adjust something or below to refer to the chart.

There is a strap under the tiller attached to a slider on deck that can be set up if needed to act as a damper and self-centraliser, but the final adjustments of this gear are always a matter of trial and error to find the exact settings to keep her steady in any given set of conditions.

Much has been said about the use of sea anchors for riding out storms in small boats. We solemnly carried a large one of

The Technical Side

these the whole way from England to America without ever using it. In fact it is rather doubtful that it would have been effective for its purpose of keeping *Sopranino's* head into the seas, since she had considerable windage forward while the lateral resistance was centred further aft.

In practice we found that such a light boat will lie to under bare poles in very rough weather with her helm lashed down to leeward, riding comfortably over the seas and taking no harm, while making some half-knot leeway.

Occasionally a sea will catch her just at the moment when it is on the point of breaking and it will break over her with an impressive roar, but without doing any damage. And since she is completely watertight above decks no water comes below at all.

Possibly in very extreme conditions it might be advisable to run off before the wind, trailing warps in a loop from quarter to quarter, to keep down the speed through the water, but though we went through severe gales in the Bay of Biscay and strong tropical squalls off Cuba we never found weather in which she would not lie to on her own in comfort.

A word on seasickness. Both of us were subject to this pest to a certain degree, usually being sick the first day out on each run, but we found that much can be done to minimise its effects. For a start, all forms of drugs can be discarded. Their effect is necessarily limited to a few hours and it would not be practical to take repeated doses over long periods, apart from the fact that most of them have a tendency to make the user sleepy, a condition which could be highly dangerous at sea at night.

Before setting out on a run it is wise to give up red meat and alcohol for three days. Then immediately before the start a good, filling meal of plain simple food should be taken. These two precautions alone are a great help.

At sea the trick seems to be to avoid rapid changes of position when you are feeling queasy. When woken up, one should lie still in one's bunk for a minute before slowly rising to a sitting position. A minute or two like that will allow one time to adjust oneself to the change of relative motion before moving to the midships seat where one can sit and dress to go on deck.

Finally one comes to a standing position in the hatch and pauses for a minute there before going on deck to take over. Naturally in an emergency one rushes on deck, is sick, and gets on with the job in hand, but if one has a few moments to spare it is much more pleasant.

NAVIGATION

The ordinary hundred-mile run or race is largely a matter of pilotage, with such comparatively short periods between departures from one coast and landfall on the next that—so long as you make a careful note of your course, distance run, leeway, drift, etc., at least every four hours—normal D.R. methods will put you down within acceptable limits.

For this purpose we carried two compasses, one a grid-steering aircraft type mounted below the bridge deck under a Perspex panel, and the other a standard hand bearing instrument, normally kept in its holder on the after side of the mast in the cabin.

As soon as we were out at sea we would normally check one against the other, just to make sure all was well, and then sail entirely on the grid, keeping the hand bearing for its normal purpose of taking bearings on landmarks and the like for obtaining coastal fixes.

If, however, the main compass should be damaged, the other would always be available as a spare to bring the ship home. For the long voyage we carried a third one, stowed safely away, as a final insurance.

Then there would be the usual charts, tide tables, tidal-stream charts, pilot books, signal-code books, and such items as foghorn, bell, and whistle. This last item, by the way, has sundry special uses, as in the taking of radio bearings, and as an additional safety precaution it should be worn around the neck of the man on watch at night in case he gets into difficulties.

In a small boat, where conditions are sometimes cramped,

The Technical Side

a large 8- or 10-inch circular protractor is useful as an alternative to the standardpa rallel rulers for taking off bearings. Also, conditions do arise from time to time where it is awkward to see the chart table and for this purpose a piece of marine plywood that one can place on one's knees as a mobile chart board is very handy.

As soon, however, as one sets out to make extended offshore passages, astro-navigation becomes essential. For the ocean crossing we carried an ordinary secondhand mate's sextant, which proved to be rugged, though of course it was treated with the greatest of care, and which was entirely satisfactory.

It is a very simple instrument, easily checked any clear night on a star and readily adjustable if any error should be found in it. With it we obtained good results, working from a position wedged in the main hatch, even in rough weather. In fact our tests showed that in average-to-rough ocean conditions a set of six sights taken close together would reveal our position to within a couple of miles.

We used the R.A.F. Tables, which are so well laid out that the business of working out a sight is no more difficult than adding up a grocery bill.

For a chronometer we used a good secondhand deck watch that turned out to be quite reliable, maintaining a steady rate for months on end; the cabin clock was a second and older deck watch that could have been pressed into service as a reserve chronometer if the main one had been upset in any way.

Once a week we would check the chronometer against the time signals received over the radio, keeping a record of the results in the back of the log book for easy reference.

The radio was a small set operated off its own dry batteries, which lasted over five months each. It gave us time signals, weather forecast, news, and entertainment, while on top of it was mounted a direction-finding loop for navigation purposes.

This last, of course, must be regarded as an aid to other means of navigation, not a substitute for them, but as an aid it has considerable value. It can be used to obtain a fix from three or four stations at one time or, in conjunction with the sextant, if only one radio beacon is available, it will give you a useful rough position.

Handling it is largely a matter of practice and skill, and it must always be remembered clearly that it can give false readings, particularly where the beam crosses a coast at an angle or in the vicinity of high cliffs. If, however, its limitations are kept well in mind all the time, it can be a most valuable piece of equipment, particularly in thick weather.

PREPARATION

By far the most important factor in determining the successful outcome of any long voyage in a small boat is the preparation for it. Right from the initial design, through the building of the boat and choice of crew and equipment, to the final loading aboard of stores, it is the unceasing and meticulous attention to every tiny detail that matters.

When the boat sails on a passage nine-tenths of the work is over. For before she leaves on her voyage, and again before she starts out on each individual passage, every conceivable thing that can by the remotest chance happen must be carefully considered, the equipment prepared to meet it, and an agreement come to between the members of the crew as to exactly how it is to be tackled.

It is not enough to provide one answer or one set of equipment to meet each condition. There must be a second and preferably a third answer prepared and ready, in case some other unforeseen factor intervenes or the first answer fails to work for some reason.

Way at the top of the list come the crew. In nine cases out of ten, when such an expedition goes wrong it is the crew that are at fault. Either they turn out to be insufficiently experienced or they fall out among themselves. In this latter respect the small boat with a crew of only two men has a considerable advantage, since they rarely see one another at sea and have nobody else with whom to take sides.

Between them, the crew must be able to undertake any job

that may need to be done, while both of them must be able to take full charge of the sailing and navigation of the vessel and to bring her safely into port if one of them should be disabled.

On the personal side, we in *Sopranino* had the great advantage of not knowing each other too well. This helps a great deal, as you remain slightly strangers throughout and therefore always on your best behaviour.

Having selected the best possible crew, the next stage is to agree on a clear and definite division of responsibilities between them. Each of us was sole and absolute arbiter in his own field. If Colin said the bottom must be scrubbed, it was scrubbed. If Patrick said the course to be steered was due west, then due west we went. There was never any argument.

After the boat has been built and the crew organised, every detail of equipment and stores must be carefully considered. For every smallest item there must be a spare or an alternative, together with the tools and means of attaching it, all perpetually kept clean and in good working order and stowed where they can be found at a moment's notice.

You pick up a tin of beans and consider it. It is going to be stowed where it may get wet, so you strip off its label and paint it all over. Then you paint 'Beans' on it in a contrasting colour. Finally you put it on a check list and stow it where it cannot damage anything else and nothing else can damage it. From time to time you check it and every now and then you take it out and examine it. Finally one day you eat the beans, throw the tin away and cross it off the check list. That job is done. And that goes for every single one of the several hundred items aboard the ship.

It is for this reason that on our voyage we always spent more time in port working to prepare for the next passage, than the passage itself actually took.

ORGANISATION

Apart from the time spent on design, building, and trial runs in *Sopranino*, we spent a clear three months on preparation

Sopranino

before we left England. Then, on the voyage from England to Miami, we took about 300 days. Of those, some 100 were spent actually sailing and 65 were holidays—far less, incidentally than the total of week-ends in the same period—leaving approximately 135 days spent on maintenance and preparation.

Thus the percentages were: preparation 45 per cent, sailing 33 per cent, and resting 22 per cent of the total days. If you add in even half of the initial three months' preparation, the figures come to: preparation 52 per cent, sailing 28 per cent, resting 20 per cent. And these figures still include no allowance for the time spent on preparatory work in the design, building, and trials stages.

Of course this expedition, in which we were setting out to prove the possibilities of an entirely new type of boat, was an extreme case, but it does serve to illustrate the importance that we attached to preparation.

Apart from preparation, information, communications, and money present the greatest problems on a long journey of this kind.

Much information may be gathered by reference to obvious sources such as doctors and dentists, and well-known organisations such as the Geographical and Zoological Societies.

Then one can consult various technical experts such as designers and discuss local details in distant places with those who have been there recently.

But there are still likely to be vast gaps in one's knowledge. A complete set of charts, including ocean wind and current charts and detail charts of all ports and harbours likely to be visited, is essential and should be collected before the start of the voyage, as charts are frequently not available even in comparatively large ports.

Then to fill the last gaps as far as possible one should make a point of consulting the local yachtsmen and ship's masters at each port along the route for further details on the next immediate passage. From these latter sources one is likely to get much contradictory information, but it is usually possible to sort it out for oneself.

The Technical Side

In foreign ports the consul and the secretary of the yacht club will usually provide much useful local detail, besides putting one on to other individuals and organisations who may be able to give one further leads. Of course all this chasing around takes time and energy, but it is a necessary part of the work of running the expedition.

Communications are always a very great problem, as one is hardly ever in one place long enough to receive answers to mail sent to one's home country, with the result that letters chase one over the face of the earth for weeks or months before finally catching up, by which time they are quite out of date as all the conditions have changed.

The best plan is to have a contact at home to whom all mail can be sent, where it is collected and kept ready for mailing to you. As soon as you arrive at a port where you intend to stay for awhile, a cable home will bring forward the current batch of mail. At the same time the home contact can send out local post-cards to all interested parties, informing them of your whereabouts.

Sometimes we had mail forwarded to the next port, but this presupposes that you will get there and may possibly be considered as tempting fate too far.

Parcels are frequently very difficult to clear through the various authorities and one way and another they are hardly worth while except in special circumstances.

We did attempt to maintain contact with England through a chain of amateur radio stations, but in fact they never once got through when the time came, so we gave them up.

In principle the home contact should be instructed always to forward mail through the local consuls or equivalent authorities wherever possible. They are usually charming and long-suffering people who are willing to forward it on to you at your next port, or better still to your next port but one, so that in the end you are likely to get most of it.

We have never yet met an ocean voyager who did not run into money troubles, more often sooner than later. A good scheme is to place funds before one leaves in the hands of the home contact or a reliable lawyer. The whole project should be discussed with him in detail and arrangements made for small sums to be sent forward to await collection at selected ports along the route. This has a remarkable effect on the speed with which one reaches those ports, apart from anything else.

Then if he retains a 'kitty', a cable will usually bring forward additional small sums within four or five days, so long as there are no currency problems involved. If there are, then the whole thing becomes much more difficult and requires even more careful planning.

From our experience it seems that no reliance should be placed on earning money en route by taking jobs locally. We did in fact do a couple of jobs and sell a few articles, but in general we found that we spent what we earned in the time it took us to earn it, so we were no better off.

Also, from what we gathered on our way around, such voyages have been known to come to an end because of the voyagers' taking jobs ashore to earn money, during which time their boat got out of order, and finally they reached a condition from which they were never able to extricate themselves.

In planning our expedition we first chose the route and then fixed on a series of bases. These were ports at which we would definitely call, whatever happened, and where we intended to stay for some time for maintenance work. This facilitated the maintenance of contact and communications all around.

The route we took was largely determined by the predicted weather conditions, turning out in fact to be the same as the old sailing ships took for the same reasons. Broadly it consisted of four distinct phases: 1800 miles south from England to the Canaries, against the prevailing southwesterly winds; then 2700 miles across the Atlantic Ocean to the West Indies; another 2500 through the islands to Florida; and 1200 up the coast to New York.

The advantage of this route over the direct one was that it gave us the trade winds for the crossing, leaving us with smaller hops to make in the less favourable latitudes, though of course it was very much longer.

The Technical Side

Once the route was decided, bases were chosen. Starting from home base in London we first made our preparations at a south-coast port conveniently near, later establishing our final base in England at Falmouth, on the very western end of the country.

Lisbon was chosen as the last base in Europe on account of its good communications with England. Then Las Palmas, in the Canaries, as our final base in the eastern hemisphere.

On the other side, Barbados was the arrival base, followed by Miami and our destination, New York. On the whole these turned out to be satisfactory. Naturally many calls were made at other intervening ports, but in every case our object was to get on to the next base with the minimum delay.

Ideally such an expedition should be planned so that you leave England in July, before the southwesterly gales set in, cross over the ocean in midwinter, clear of the hurricane season and follow the sun up to New York. That, in principle, was what we planned to do.

In fact, there were delays, so that we did not get away until early September and had to fight our way south through gales and calms to Portugal. But the conditions were still favourable for the crossing and for the run through the islands to Miami. There we had more delays, with the result that it was a matter of bucking the northeasters up Chesapeake Bay and the last part of the run to New York. But such things are to be expected in an undertaking like this. However carefully you plan you will eventually have to accept last-minute modifications and compromises.

STORES

The most important commodity aboard a small boat at sea is water. The average healthy man can exist up to about fourteen days without food, but without water he is liable to die within four.

It is very heavy, so that it is essential to carry neither too much nor too little. We allowed ourselves one imperial quart per man per day, for all purposes, and found that this was about right. For each individual passage we estimated rather conservatively our running time and carried water for that time plus 50 per cent, in case of emergencies. The weight, by the way, of one quart of water is $2\frac{1}{2}$ pounds.

If you use a single water tank and it leaks, you are likely to lose the lot. So we carried ours in a hundred aluminium bottles, each about one foot high by four inches across, with a rubber-sealed screw top. These held one quart each and we filled as many as were required for each passage. The empty ones were of course spare buoyancy.

In addition to safeguarding us against the loss of water supply, these small containers had the advantage that they made it easy to count and ration our water, while the weight could be suitably distributed over the ship and they eliminated any possibility of surging or movement of the weight at sea.

On several occasions we ran into trouble because of drinking water that had been recommended to us but which in fact made us very ill. In many foreign countries the ordinary water supplies simply are not safe to drink. Local advice is frequently misleading, since the locals have had time to build up a resistance to it.

There are two satisfactory answers to this problem. You can use ordinary water and boil every drop of it for three minutes before use, a system which has the disadvantage that if your stove breaks down or you run out of fuel for it you lose the use of your water supply. Better, you can fill up your drinking-water containers with one of the gassy spring waters that come in bottles. These taste odd but they are generally absolutely safe and if kept in airtight containers will remain good for as long as four months.

Next comes the question of food. The average man needs a total of 2 lbs. 12 ozs. a day. Pills and concentrates have their uses, but he still needs that much bulk if he is to keep fit and efficient. We based our allowances of food on the estimated number of days for each passage plus 25 per cent, since in an

The Technical Side

emergency rations can be reduced below the stand ard figure without serious effects.

The quantities of each individual item carried were based on more or less standard meals—so many breakfasts, so many lunches, etc. For this purpose, where the object of the food is to keep the men healthy, a dull but safe standard diet is acceptable, with a few small luxuries thrown in as an afterthought to break up the monotony.

Breakfast was based on a bowl of porridge or cornflakes each, a tin of beans or spaghetti between two men, fresh fruit when possible, plus Nescafé or cocoa, sugar, tinned milk, Ryvita, tinned butter, and marmalade.

Sugar is good value, giving immediate energy, and we always carried a generous allowance of it. Ryvita was carried as a substitute for bread on journeys of over four days. The evaporated type of tinned milk has many more uses and is generally more satisfactory than the condensed variety.

For lunch we allowed a tin of soup between two men, plus Ryvita and something to put on it, such as sardines, pickles, cheese, or tinned fish. Plus more coffee.

Tea again was a light meal of biscuits and coffee, plus any cakes that were available.

Supper in the evening was the main meal of the day. For this we allowed two bowls each of basic stew, made from tinned corned beef, tinned peas or beans, tomato juice, fresh onions, served with fresh potatoes. After that, one small tin of fruit between two men is nice if it is available, and of course more coffee.

These meals, though uninteresting, proved perfectly efficient for their purpose, and we did in fact arrive across the ocean after twenty-eight days at sea fitter than when we started.

It is, however, highly desirable to provide good supplies of sweets and biscuits for the man on watch,es pecially at night, as it helps to keep him awake besides giving him some little extra to add colour to his diet.

Then of course there are the personal items of clothing, plus bedding, towels, washing gear, and the like. These again

Sopranino

require careful consideration in order to provide for all contingencies with a minimum of weight and bulk aboard.

When a little boat arrives in a strange port, particularly abroad, the inhabitants take a quick look to decide for themselves what sort of a set-up it is. Nine out of ten of them have no clues as to what it is all about, so they have a strong tendency to make a snap judgment based on outward appearance.

It is therefore of the first importance to arrive in port looking as smart as possible. You cannot hope to keep your clothes smart and tidy in a storm at sea, but what you can do is to have at least one set each of neat and suitable clothing for use in port.

These clothes, for two men, can be packed in a spray-proof suitcase which in turn can be wrapped in two waterproof rubber bags and slung from the deckhead in the driest part of the cabin, which in our case was forward between the bunks.

Then, on arrival at a port, you can heave to in a quiet spot near the dock at which you intend to land, to clean up and change into your shore-going clothes for the arrival.

Before making a passage you arrange all your stores in neat piles in a store ashore, if you can find one, to check them over. Seen like that, it is quite impossible to believe that they will ever all go into the boat. Great piles of tins, heaps of clothing and bedding, dozens and dozens of items of equipment of every awkward shape and size fill a large room, while row upon row of water-pots line the walls. And all this has to be stowed where it will be available when it is needed.

Stowage followed a set plan with us. First one would pack the after locker with paints and varnishes, warps and fenders, everything that was not liable to damage if it should get damp and which was not likely to be needed under way.

Then the ready-use food lockers under the galley and chart table were filled with a selection of food and water-cans and pots for immediate use. More water-pots were stowed under the seat and the remainder or reserve supplies were stowed each side of the cockpit in the main storage lockers.

On top of these last were stowed the sail bags, together with odd bags of equipment that might be required in a hurry, with the thought in mind that no ferrous metals must come within three feet of the compass.

Bedding was stowed at the forward ends of the bunks, while personal sea clothing was stowed in net racks which extended upward from the bunks to the deckhead. More net racks were fitted under the deck beams to hold books and papers, and finally each man had a small personal locker at the foot of his bunk.

When at the last moment you are faced with an awkward and tiresome item such as a pot of glue without a lid or perhaps a half-unravelled ball of string, the standard procedure, if you can get away with it, is to slip it into your partner's personal locker. Acrimony will result, of course, if he finds it, but there is always a good chance that you may make the next port before it is transferred to your own locker.

In theory the cockpit should be kept clear, though when cruising we always kept the main anchor and a warp stowed at the after end of it and on the Atlantic run we put an extra four one-gallon cans of spare water there as well, besides lashing a crate of tomatoes over the after hatch, but that was a special case.

We had one unusual stowage problem on that run which cropped up right at the last minute. Some kind friend had asked us if we would like a bunch of bananas. To the uninitiated like us that meant a dozen or so, so we accepted gladly.

When the thing turned up it was cylindrical in shape, with a stout stalk down the middle and well over a hundred bananas arranged in clusters around it. In all it was some four feet tall by eighteen inches across and weighed all of forty pounds. There was only one place it would go and that was in one of the bunks, so we took it in turns to sleep in the other one while we lived on an unvarying diet of bananas, bananas, and more bananas until they were finished.

COLIN'S SECOND THOUGHTS

It is always of interest to look back on a cruise or race and to think in what ways it could have been improved and what

Sopranino

could be altered to advantage for next time. This is, I think, of especial interest with *Sopranino* who is a little unorthodox. The comments that I make here are my own personal opinions and I dare say that Patrick will disagree with many of them. So little went wrong that we can only guess really at improvements.

First, the boat in general. It will be of little surprise to you that I consider *Sopranino* to be below the optimum size for an ocean cruiser, but it may well be of interest to know by how very little.

At sea she proved an admirable and completely adequate vehicle which catered comfortably for all your basic wants. Although she has little below, what is there is not cramped or pinched in any way. A full-size and dry bunk, a full-size galley, a full-size chart table, and a stock of dry clothes; what could anybody desire more when offshore? On deck the sail plan and gear is of such small size that the man on watch can, all by himself, cope with almost any situation that arises. Not only is this most satisfying for the man off watch but the man on watch feels pleasantly in complete control, and it is almost impossible to tire the crew with sail changing or sheeting. Tired crews have probably been the cause of more disasters to sailing yachts than the failure of anything else. *Sopranino* is so light in displacement that she comes to little harm should she broach to when running before a strong breeze, a major danger for larger yachts.

Again, *Sopranino* carries a crew of two—which must be the best possible number. So many ocean cruises seem to degenerate into a wrangle amongst the crew. With two only you see so little of the other fellow that you are always pleased to see him when you do. After you have both slept for eight hours and spent another two hours each below, dressing and so on, there are only four hours of the day left in which to see each other. Less, probably, than you see of the next man at the office.

Another major cause of failure of ocean voyages is the underestimating of the expenses. It is a point to make for *Sopranino-*

The Technical Side

sized craft that they probably are amongst the cheapest to keep in first-rate condition. I would not pretend that 'Soppers' is the optimum size, for her very smallness made maintenance afloat the more awkward. On the other hand she is too small to need expensive slipping to do the bottom. Almost any crane will lift her out of the water and if there is not a crane she can as easily be careened.

At sea, as I have said, she is nearly perfect, but could with advantage be a few inches longer to give a slightly bigger cockpit and a separate stowage for wet oilskins below.

In harbour she is too small. We lived on board for the best part of a year without trouble, but it would have been so much more pleasant if we could both have sat up in the cabin together to write our letters and do the small jobs about the house when it was raining outside.

In harbour she is too delicate and vulnerable. There are comparatively few yacht harbours and most of our time in port was spent in the company of barges and commercial boats. *Sopranino* is too light and delicate to hold her own in such company and we had to watch over her constantly. Still, with the advantages of that light construction at sea I would on a next time be prepared to put up with the disadvantages in harbour. I would, however, surround her with an enormous and possibly pneumatic rubber fender. I have in mind the kind of thing that the tenders to flying boats have. The loss of speed at sea from this thing would be negligible if we were cruising.

In harbour you are reduced to local standards for outside help with the boat. This means that you must learn to do as much as possible yourself, and of course it is no more than good seamanship. However, for such things as the charging of batteries you are forced to rely on outside help. Now those that we had were fine batteries designed for aerobatic aircraft and altogether very special. Unfortunately they also required a special charging rate and specific gravity different from that of the normal car battery. This was always a source of fuss. The unusual charging rates had invariably to be explained to a dumb garage-hand whose language we did not have and who

217

Sopranino

thought he knew all about batteries anyway. The moral of this is that equipment which has to rely on shore maintenance should be of the level of the most backward port at which you are likely to call.

In general, I would, if I were to design for myself my ideal ocean cruiser, at the moment draw one of much the same style as *Sopranino* but about four feet longer—the minimum increase in size to give me my comfort in harbour.

If now we were to set about doing the same thing again in the same boat I would make the following changes:

Firstly, I would not cut her rig down by quite so much. With the weight of stores in her *Sopranino* proved to be stiffer than I had expected and we could have had a mast two or three feet taller without risk of her tipping over when you climbed to its top. The extra sail would have been very welcome in light airs, the time when *Sopranino* is most vulnerable. We might have had to do a little more sail-changing, but that would not have done us any harm.

Secondly, I would not take so much with us. Ellam, as you will have gathered, never does things by halves and we had everything on board. Many things proved to be not worth the space they took up and the trouble of getting round them or past them to the things we did need. I would list such things as bottles of ink and blotting paper and luggage labels. Also some of the equipment that we did not use, like the foredeck awning and the wind tube, a vast canvas tube which when hoisted to the masthead sent great gales of wind into the cabin. In my own particular department I would halve the number of tools and paint pots and brushes and cutlasses. The optimum equipment level is, I am convinced, about midway between Patrick's lavishness and my original rather Spartan ideas.

Next time I would send food out to ports along the way to be cached until we got there. We more or less took our whole supply with us from Falmouth to last us for six months. I would rather have food cached along the way and be certain of it than additional supplies of money to buy it, as and when. I would not have on board more than about two months' supply.

Next time, too, we would spend less time in harbour. With the experience we now have, time spent on maintenance could be cut to about half and I think that probably applies to the paper work as well. Apart from any other reason, time spent in port is unduly expensive. Patrick will agree with me when I guess that the cost of living on board in harbour, living as if in a small tent, and very modestly at that, worked out at about £15 a week as against £4 a week when at sea. This for two of us, a boat, and our pink elephant.

Again, as Patrick has said, we would not attempt to earn an honest shilling on the way, for it invariably cost the whole of what we made to live while we did it, and the net result was a falling behind on our schedule.

It was part of the object of the voyage to have a look at as many harbours as possible. Having seen them we would not call at many of them again. We could make longer passages. Once you are two days out, time in days means nothing whatsoever and a ten-day passage is no more arduous than a three-day voyage. I would put a working maximum of twelve days for a passage involving mainly windward work if the crew are to remain in top condition. Downwind, with self-steering doing the. work, we could have kept at sea for another month.

The layout below proved to be admirable, but of course we could now improve it in detail. I would like a stowage for wet oilskins between the chart table and the starboard (Patrick's) bunk. I would improve the access to the lockers by making the top of the chart table hinge and by making bigger holes into the cockpit side lockers. Between the bunks I would build a much bigger waterproof box in which I would keep everything from the vegetables to Patrick's socks. At the foot of the bunks, either between them or flat against the bulkhead, I would build a hanging locker for our shore-going clothes to make them more accessible. But before I did any of these, I would make provision in the cockpit to raise our bottoms above the water that swirled around them. I have in mind something soft and pneumatic.

Sopranino

On deck I would cut maintenance by a much more extensive use of stainless steel and anodised aluminium for fittings and rigging.

There is no reason why we should not be able to steer *Sopranino* from inside. A short rod to connect with the quadrant would keep us so very much more dry in bad weather. Standing in the hatch we would keep warm and much drier. A simple apron would keep water from getting below.

I would have canvas jackets for all the varnish work—to protect some of it from the sun and salt at sea and some of it from the feet of visitors in harbour. And I should have mosquito nets covering the hatch to increase our privacy, not only from the mosquito but from the curious sightseers who used to peer down the hatch at us as we lay in our bunks.

But I couldn't ask for a better skipper and you get to know your fellow-man rather well on this sort of lark.

SOME SPECIAL SKILLS FOR SOPRANAUTS

How to Get into Your Bunk

This is easy. First, assume a sitting position on the toilet, facing forward, and squirm out of your clothing. If you feel something warm and clammy, don't worry: it only means you have put your hand in the stew. It'll probably improve it.

Now grasp the beam over your head with both hands, kick your legs into the air and straighten out smartly. If you fetch up in the wrong bunk it means that you didn't time the roll of the ship right, but you are all right where you are, so why fuss? If, on the other hand, you land with your head down the toilet, you haven't got the knack. You are supposed to push at the end of the swing, not pull.

Let us assume for the moment that you have done it right. You are now flat on your back in your bunk. Or nearly flat. There is an excruciating pain halfway up your spine. Your partner, kindly soul, has left the sextant there. The next sight you take with that thing is going to be a honey.

You transfer it to his bunk. Now to get your blanket. It is

The Technical Side

sitting neatly rolled by your feet. If you try to sit up and reach it you will stun yourself on the deck beam, which is a quick way of going to sleep but you'll wake up feeling cold. Better to clasp it between your toes and ease it towards you. Not too far, or your knees will jam against the deck and you will have to shout for help to be released.

Now wriggle it up between your legs and your bunk, after the manner of a python digesting his breakfast, until you can clasp it between your fingers, drag it up beside you and roll over, one complete turn. This will wrap it around you, more or less. True, there will be an icy draught somewhere around your kidneys, but that is one of the inevitable Laws of Nature and there is nothing you can do about it. You may as well try and get some sleep before it's your watch on deck again.

How to Read the Barometer

First, clear your bunk of all pots, pans, instruments, and wet clothing. Then take your pencil and paper and throw them down to the end. Next draw your feet up underneath you, lean forward on the toilet seat, wait for the ship to roll the right way and do a shallow headlong dive. Correctly done, this will send you sliding up to the far end of your bunk, where the barometer is situated.

Incorrectly done, it will leave you with your head through the radio loop and your feet in the stew, but let's not think of that. From here on there are two techniques. Either you can curve your back, rearing up to stare at the thing a couple of inches away, or better, you can roll over on your back and read it backwards in a mirror.

Now you really do have a problem on your hands. Getting out. This is hard to describe, but the only way is to ease yourself down, inch by inch, until you land with a bump on the floor with your feet on the toilet, your back against the mast, sitting in a puddle of water. Next, pass your feet through the galley and plant them firmly on your partner's pillow. Grasp the ceiling, straighten your knees and there you are, back in position Number One, on the toilet seat. If you have left the pencil and paper behind, you simply go through the same routine to get them back.

How to Find a Tin of Stew

Starting from Position Number One, you will find that you cannot get your left hand into the left-hand locker, unless your arm happens to have an extra joint somewhere between the wrist and the elbow. But you *can* get your right hand into it by passing your arm between your thighs and under your left knee.

Through the small opening, the locker is crammed full of tins. Tins of peas, tins of milk, tins of spinach. Even nameless and anonymous tins that someone forgot to mark. And somewhere among them are tins of stew. A Very Skilled Expert can tell by the feel of a tin what's inside it, but for the beginner it means taking them out, one by one.

When you have a nice large pile of them on the floor the ship will lurch and down they will come on your bare feet. But you must press on, and eventually you will come to a whole vein of stew. You place one aside and start putting all the other tins back again. You are crafty this time and put a couple of stews where you can find them next time. You won't, of course, but it was a nice try.